PREPPER'S GUIDE TO KNOTS

The 100 Most Useful Tying Techniques for Surviving any Disaster

Scott Finazzo

Ulysses Press

Published in the U.S. by
ULYSSES PRESS
P.O. Box 3440
Berkeley, CA 94703
www.ulyssespress.com

ISBN: 978-1-61243-598-5
Library of Congress Control Number 2016934498

Printed in the United States by United Graphics, Inc.

10 9 8 7 6 5 4 3 2 1

Acquisitions Editor: Casie Vogel
Managing Editor: Claire Chun
Project Editor: Bridget Thoreson
Editor: Bill Cassel
Proofreader: Lauren Harrison
Front cover/interior design and layout: what!design @ whatweb.com
Cover artwork: knot photographs © Amy Wewers; red background © Eky Studio/shutterstock.com; rope illustration © maritime_m/shutterstock.com; knot icon © Kilroy79.eps/shutterstock.com; house icon © zelimirz.eps/shutterstock.com; cross icon © tulpahn/shutterstock.com; cloud icon © Crystal Home/shutterstock.com
Interior artwork: knot photos © Amy Wewers; rope illustration © maritime_m/shutterstock.com

Distributed by Publishers Group West

CONTENTS

INTRODUCTION

There is something awe-inspiring about seeing a person who is proficient at working with rope. Whatever the purpose may be—tying something down, hoisting something up, or any of a thousand other random reasons—watching a skilled person take a length of rope and manipulate it is not dissimilar to watching an artist paint. It demands respect at the same time that it creates a hint of envy. Underlying the beauty of knotcraft is the functionality of it: Knots are works of art that have a practical application. Their purpose is to make some aspect of life easier.

As long as humans have been walking the Earth, vines and strands of whatever material is available have been braided to create rope to pull, drag, hoist, and carry anything and everything. There is evidence of knots being used dating all the way back to the time of cave dwellers. As humankind has progressed knots have been used in construction, boating, fishing, farming, and just about any other application you can imagine.

Ropes and knots played major roles in the construction of some of the world's greatest man-made structures. The pyramids of Egypt, the Roman Colosseum, and the Great Wall of China are just a few examples of what can be accomplished with very little technology by maximizing the strength of rope and reaping the benefits of the mechanical advantage it affords.

Humans have been to the highest and lowest points on this planet thanks, in part, to ropes and knots. The deepest caves and the peak of Mount Everest were only conquered because ropes and knots enabled people and equipment to ascend and descend, and to do so safely.

> "Time really seemed to pass even though I was falling clear and I realized that unless the rope came tight fairly soon, I would come to a rather sticky end on the bottom of the crevasse."
>
> — *Sir Edmund Hillary on Mount Everest*

While knots have certainly evolved over time, many knots have enduring characteristics that render them just as effective today as they were hundreds or even thousands of years ago. Knotcraft is a rare clash of nostalgia and the contemporary. Though knots have been used throughout history, the earliest known books on knots are the formal manuals on seamanship written around 1800. Since then, there has been a great deal of literature on the subject. Perhaps the most famous is the 1944 publication *The Ashley Book of Knots,* which was written by author, artist, sailor, and knot expert Clifford W. Ashley. It includes over 2,000 knots with over 7,000 illustrations and has been heralded as the bible of knots.

With all of the other books on knots out there, especially one as inclusive as Ashley's, why another one? Why this one? Allow me to explain. I have been an adventurous and outdoorsy type of person all of my life. Having climbed mountains and wandered out into and across the ocean, I am familiar with the uses and benefits of tying knots. I have also been a firefighter for nearly 20 years and for almost 15 of those years I have been a rope rescue technician. In that capacity I have been trained to utilize ropes and knots in the most critical of all environments: life safety. I have also written several books on disaster preparation and response. *The Prepper's Workbook* helps the reader prepare for disaster, and *The Neighborhood Emergency Response Handbook* and *Prepper's Survival Medicine Handbook* are guides on what to do after a catastrophe.

Factoring in all of those things, my goal for this book, *The Prepper's Guide to Knots,* is to ensure that you are prepared to tie knots when the need arises. When you need a knot for a specific purpose, there is nothing quite like being able to tie it. Simply tying the right knot at the right time affords you a feeling of accomplishment and confidence, over and above the practical use of the knot.

With this in mind I've chosen 100 knots that are common, practical, easy to tie, easy to remember, and useful in critical situations. This book will teach you how to tie them and when to use them.

You won't necessarily want or need to learn them all; a handful of knots can get you by in most situations. But if you're the sort of person who appreciates preparation, for whom just knowing the basics isn't enough, this book will provide you with a variety of tested and practical options.

Whether you want to join two ropes together (bends), attach something to a rope (hitches), stop unraveling (stopper knots), bind something (binding knots), or create a loop (loops), this book will show you several knots that can accomplish whatever task you are facing. The way to truly be prepared is to learn at least a few knots to accomplish each task and a way to tie them that is comfortable for you and easy to remember.

Knot proficiency will only come with repetition. Get a length of rope at least a couple of feet long that is supple enough to enable you to easily tie knots, and keep it accessible. When there is downtime at work or at home, or if you are just sitting around watching television, tie some knots. Tie variations of the knots. Learn new ways to tie the knots you already know. It's a simple way to learn during your leisure time that reaps significant benefits when the time comes. By repeatedly tying knots you develop muscle memory, and before you know it, you can quickly tie the knots you need without having to really think about it.

In addition to tying your own knots, being able to recognize a well-tied knot can be extremely useful. My friend, fellow firefighter, sailing buddy, and rope guru Kent Saturday taught me years ago that when you are the person who is going to be hanging by a rope off of a rooftop, tower, or cliff, you will want to be able to look at every knot before you go over, recognize it, and know if it is tied correctly.

Knotcraft is an ancient art that is still practical in our everyday lives. Even if you have no intention of sailing across the ocean or scaling a mountain, ropes and knots have virtually limitless uses and applications, particularly in a situation that eliminates technology and forces you to revert to rudimentary tools and skills. There are no negatives to being skilled with ropes and knots.

Learn, practice, demonstrate, enjoy, repeat.

MATERIALS USED IN ROPES

Rope is made from two sources: natural fibers and synthetic fibers. Until the advent and spread of synthetic materials in the 1940s, natural fiber was the primary type of rope used. Historically natural-fiber rope materials such as cotton, hemp, manila hemp, sisal, and jute have been readily available and inexpensive. Today, however, synthetic materials like nylon and polyester are more widely used.

NATURAL FIBERS

While natural-fiber rope is often softer and more absorbent than synthetic, it is also relatively weak and susceptible to dry rot. Because of its strength and durability issues, it is more often used in utility-type applications such as flagpoles, tents, pet products, and hammocks. Natural-fiber rope is also often used in landscaping decoration, handrails, or other ornamentation because it is visually attractive.

COTTON: Cotton rope is soft and pliable. Because of its low strength it is primarily used as decoration or in other applications that do not involve life safety, such as flagpoles and extension-ladder halyards. Cotton rope is very susceptible to damage and abrasion and should be carefully inspected on a regular basis.

HEMP: Hemp rope was used when sailing ships were in their prime. It was soaked in pine tar to help compensate for its propensity to dry rot. Hemp is one of the strongest natural ropes in the world but was phased out when manila, which is less prone to dry rot, became widely available.

MANILA HEMP: Manila hemp is not actually hemp at all, but was given the name when it was brought forward to replace hemp as the primary component of rope. The fibers used to make manila hemp rope actually come from the abacá plant (which is in the banana family); it is named for the capital of the Philippines, which is one of the world's main producers of abaca. Manila hemp is far superior to hemp in that it is equally flexible and durable, but resistant to salt water damage. The main disadvantage of manila hemp is that it is prone to shrinkage, which can be problematic if a knot is tied in it and then it becomes wet. New rope is often immersed in water before its first use to allow the majority of the shrinkage to occur in advance. With the popularity of synthetic rope over the last few decades, manila hemp has become less and less relevant.

CHOOSING THE RIGHT TYPE OF ROPE

Choosing the right type of rope comes down to your specific needs. There a few questions you should ask yourself to determine which is the right type of rope for you.

- What task will you be performing?
- What length of rope will you need?
- What diameter?
- Will this be a life safety application?
- Will you be working in a vertical or horizontal realm?
- Do you need strong UV resistance, chemical resistance, abrasion resistance, floating capabilities, etc.?

You may not know the answer to all of these questions. You may not even know the answer to any of them. There are many situations where any rope will do the job; but when you have a specific need, you should choose the safest and best type of rope to achieve your goal.

SISAL: For years sisal has been used as in the agricultural and shipping industries. Because it is strong, flexible, and resistant to deterioration but bristly and not very forgiving on your hands, it is popular as shipping twine, baler twine, hay binder twine, and small craft lashing, but not as rope per se. As with other natural fiber ropes, it has been slowly losing favor to synthetic rope.

JUTE: Jute is an alternative to hemp, though not as dense or strong. It is used in a lot of landscaping applications because of its biodegradable nature. As a common component of burlap, jute is used to wrap root balls and laid out to prevent erosion as natural vegetation grows. Because it is coarse, scratchy, and can become brittle, jute is not commonly used as rope, but mostly as fabric, yarn, sacks, and netting.

Natural ropes were traditionally weak and prone to dry rot. In order to make them strong enough to withstand the demands put on them, they had to be made so thick that they became unmanageable and impractical to use with equipment such as pulleys and carabiners. The 1940s saw the introduction of synthetic fibers in the manufacturing of rope.

SYNTHETIC FIBERS

Synthetic ropes such as nylon, polypropylene, and polyester offer multiple advantages over natural-fiber rope. They are stronger than natural fibers, with superior pulling and lifting strength. This is in part because they can have continuous fiber that extends the entire length of the rope, where that is not possible with natural ropes. Synthetic rope is immune to dry rot and has superior grip characteristics as well as qualities that make it more elastic and pliable.

While synthetic rope is vastly more popular today than natural-fiber ropes, there are a few disadvantages to consider. Certain types of synthetic ropes (known as "dynamic" ropes) are prone to elongation. Also, synthetic ropes begin to lose strength when exposed to temperatures above 150°F, and they melt when temperatures exceed 300°F (such as at a friction point).

While synthetic ropes are superior to natural-fiber ropes for most applications, some purists prefer to use naturally occurring fibers because synthetic ropes are petroleum-based. In life safety and rescue operations, though, synthetic ropes are used exclusively; the shortcomings of natural-fiber ropes make them too risky for these types of situations.

LAID VS. BRAIDED ROPE

In terms of construction, there are basically two types of rope: laid rope and braided rope.

Laid rope is a form of rope construction where individual fibers are made into yarns. The yarns are then twisted into threads, which are then twisted into strands. The final step is when the strands are twisted together to form rope. Historically, laid rope has been limited by the length of the materials available, but modern manufacturing allows virtually limitless length.

In laid rope the twists and counter-twists lend strength and flexibility. The valleys between the strands, which are called "lays," lie in a diagonal direction. The strands are either Z-laid (right-handed) or S-laid (left-handed). Z-laid ropes, no matter how you hold them, will appear to twist upward and to the right. S-laid ropes appear to twist upward and to the left. There is no difference in strength but, when coiling the rope, to prevent twists, Z-laid ropes should be coiled clockwise and S-laid counterclockwise.

A braided construction is common in synthetic ropes and consists of an inner core and outer protective sheath useful in high-friction situations. Braided ropes are smooth and supple, easily manipulated into knots and systems. There are several types of braided rope:

- **HOLLOW BRAID:** This kind of rope has no inner core. It is very flexible but flattens during use. Hollow braid is most often found in small-diameter rope. Its most redeeming quality is the ease with which it is spliced.

- **PARALLEL CORE:** This is very strong rope that has a braided protective sheath over a core of straight (or lightly twisted) yarns.

- **MULTIBRAID:** Multibraid is flexible and does not kink. It is braided with two pairs of Z-laid strands and two pairs of S-laid strands.

- **BRAID ON BRAID:** In this type of rope a braided core is surrounded by a braided sheath. It has less stretch and less flexibility than hollow braid, but it is the strongest—and therefore the most expensive—construction of rope.

NYLON: Nylon is an extremely popular rope with widespread use in boating, climbing, rappelling, towing, and numerous other applications. Its superior strength, smooth surface, and abrasion resistance make it ideal for winches and pulley systems. Because of all this, in addition to its elasticity and durability, nylon is the primary material used for rescue rope. The main negative to nylon rope is that it may absorb water and sink.

POLYPROPYLENE: The primary benefits of polypropylene rope are that it is cheap and it floats. It also resists rot and mildew and does a good job resisting acids, bases, and solvents. It can be made to look like a natural-fiber rope, which is appealing to those who want the look of natural fiber with the strength and durability of a synthetic rope. It is commonly used in utility applications on boats, but although it is strong, it is not strong enough to be recommended for life safety.

POLYESTER: Stiffer than nylon, polyester is also slightly stronger and, unlike nylon, does not lose its strength when wet. It also does not float. Polyester has very low stretch because the majority of stretch is removed in the manufacturing. This makes it a good alternative to nylon and polypropylene when it is being used in a static application. However, because it doesn't stretch, polyester is not a good choice if the load is subject to jerking.

CARE AND CLEANING

Rope and other cordage can be immensely useful, but as strong and durable as it may be, nearly everything from storage to cleaning to regular use can degrade it. Proper rope care is essential for reliability and long life. It is particularly important when the rope is being used in a life safety situation.

One of rope's worst enemies is sunlight. Ultraviolet (UV) degradation takes its toll, in varying degrees, on all rope (the amount of degradation depends on which type of material the rope is made from). You should take steps to store your rope out of direct sunlight. If you have rope that is subject to long-term UV exposure, such as on a boat, be sure to check the fibers regularly for damage.

Chemicals can also wreak havoc on the fibers of rope. Avoid allowing your rope to come in contact with, or storing them in close proximity to, chemicals. Even the vapors will affect the fibers of rope. Excessive heat and cold also have negative effects. Avoid allowing a wet rope to freeze, and keep it stored in a cool, dry place with low humidity.

To clean a rope, shake it free of dust and debris and brush it with a soft bristle brush. You can also wash ropes with clean, warm water and then allow them fully dry before storing them. If the rope is especially dirty, use a mild detergent and a soft bristle brush. If you use a hose, do not use a high-pressure hose; it can damage the fibers of the rope. Using a garden hose is fine. To dry the rope, don't use a mechanical dryer or any other artificial heat source. Suspend the rope and allow it to properly air dry.

Ropes should be thoroughly inspected on a regular basis, particularly if abrasive materials such as dirt, rock, or silica have been in contact with the rope. Rope used in life safety situations should be inspected after every use. It is time-consuming and tedious, but every inch should be checked for breaks, tears, cuts, degradation, and any other signs of damage. Loose, worn, and broken material are all signs of damage. A small amount of discoloration or surface fluffing is to be expected if a rope has been heavily used, but should be properly cleaned, dried, and inspected often.

TERMS

Knotcraft terminology is a little complicated. Knots are categorized by their function (hitches, loops, bends, etc.), but some knots have multiple uses. There are varying schools of thought on what to call certain knots, what their true purpose is, and even the "right" way to tie them.

Even so, there are some well-understood terms that you'll need to know when learning how to tie knots.

- **STANDING END:** The part of the rope not involved in the knot. The "standing part" lies between the knot and the standing end.

- **WORKING END:** The end of the rope that is used to tie the knot.

- **BIGHT:** A U shape made in the rope where the ends or parts do not cross.

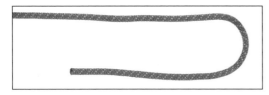

- **LOOP:** A circle formed in the rope without the crossing the ends.

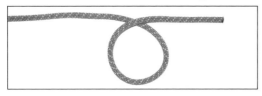

- **ROUND TURN:** A complete turn in the rope.

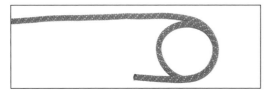

- **OVERHAND LOOP:** A loop created when the working end crosses over the standing end.

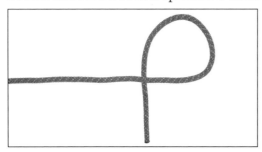

- **UNDERHAND LOOP:** A loop created when the working end crosses under the standing end.

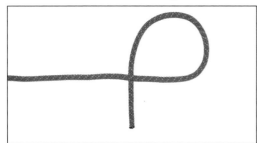

OTHER TERMS

DRESSING A KNOT: The act of arranging a knot in order to improve the knot's performance and strength.

SLIDE AND GRIP: The action of a knot continuously gripping and sliding on a rope until friction becomes strong enough to withstand the load being placed on it.

SHOCK LOAD: Technically means "a dynamically applied load greater than double the static load." Put more simply, it is a sudden or unexpected weight placed on a rope or rope system.

You will also read the term "safety" or "safety knot." When tying knots, it is common to tie an extra knot in the end of the rope (typically the working end) to make sure the end doesn't get pulled through the knot you just created. Most times a simple Overhand Knot will do (page 15).

BASIC KNOTS

In this book knots are divided into categories based on their function. When, as is often the case, a particular knot could be put into a number of different categories, I've tried to use common sense to maximize simplicity and organization.

The first section is titled "Basic Knots" because many of the knots it covers are very common and simple to tie, and also serve as the basis for many of the other knots located elsewhere in this book. Within this section you may find knots you may have been tying your whole life without knowing they had a name. There are also "stopper knots," which are tied for the purposes of preventing rope from pulling through an object or an object sliding off the rope. A good working knowledge of the knots in this section will provide you with a solid foundation for tying other, more involved knots as you progress through the book.

⚓ TIP ⚓

Oftentimes, when a knot has been used to hold a load, it can become extremely difficult to untie. Most people, at one time or another, have experienced this with their own shoelaces. There is a trick used by those who work with ropes to loosen a knot and make it easier to untie. Roll the knot between your hands as if you're rolling up cookie dough. You may have to press hard. This usually works to loosen the knot, allowing you to untie it.

OVERHAND KNOT

Also known as: *Thumb Knot*

The Overhand Knot is in the family of stopper knots. It is used to prevent a rope from pulling through an object or rope bag. It can also be used to keep objects from sliding off a rope. Whether it is used as a simple stopper knot or the basis for other, more complex knots, the Overhand Knot is easily the most commonly tied knot. Most people do not even require instruction to tie an Overhand Knot, but you must be careful when tying one. If it is tied too tightly, it can become very difficult to undo; and if it is not tied tightly enough, it can easily come undone.

1 Make a loop in the rope.

3 Pull tight.

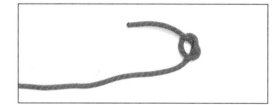

2 Tuck the working end through the loop.

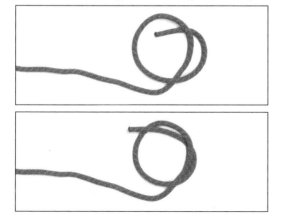

DOUBLE OVERHAND KNOT

The primary use of the Double Overhand Knot is as a bigger version of the overhand knot. If you don't feel confident that the Overhand Knot is girthy enough to serve your purpose, then a Double Overhand Knot may provide the bulk to accomplish your task. The Double Overhand Knot also is often used to tie a safety knot in the working end of other knots.

1 Tie an Overhand Knot.

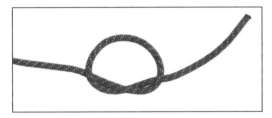

2 Tuck in the working end a second time.

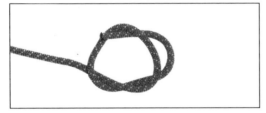

3 Pull the ends apart slightly, twisting in opposite directions. If the knot doesn't begin to form a clean knot as shown here, twist the opposite direction.

TRIPLE OVERHAND KNOT

The Triple Overhand Knot is, again, used as a larger stopper knot in a situation where you want even more girth to serve your purpose. It is also used decoratively and symbolically.

1 Tie a Double Overhand Knot.

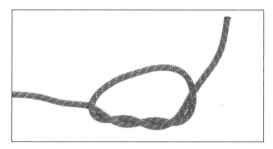

2 Tuck in the working end a third time.

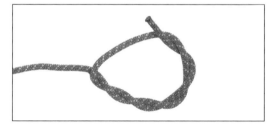

3 Pull the ends apart slightly, twisting in opposite directions.

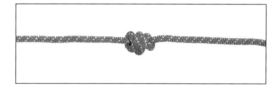

//// KNOT NOTES \\\\

Monks and nuns use this knot to weight their habits, the triple knot being a reference to their threefold sacred vows: obedience, stability, and conversion of morals.

OVERHAND KNOT
WITH A DRAWLOOP

Also known as: *Slipped Overhand Knot*

A drawloop is a bight or loop placed in a knot that can be used to attach another rope or an object or as a place to grip the rope, and can be drawn out of the knot by pulling one end of the rope.

The benefit of using an Overhand Knot with a Drawloop is that when the loop is placed around a load, it cinches the overhand knot tighter. Then, when the load is released, you can simply pull the standing end to release the knot.

1 Tie an Overhand Knot.

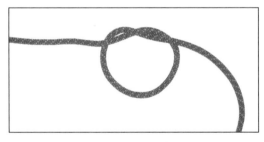

2 Tuck the working end back through the loop. Before pulling the loop all the way through, maintain the bight formed when tucking the working end back through.

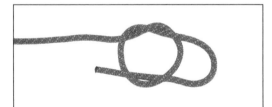

3 Pull tight.

TWO STRAND OVERHAND KNOT

Also known as: *Flat Overhand Knot, European Death Knot*

A Two Strand Overhand Knot is tied the exact same way as an Overhand Knot. It creates a larger knot than the Overhand Knot and can be used as a larger stopper knot, but is commonly used as a safety to prevent ends of the rope pulling through a knot, or for tying together the drawstrings found in swimming trunks, sweatpants, and pajamas.

1 Place the two cords together, parallel to one another.

2 Holding them together, make a loop in the rope.

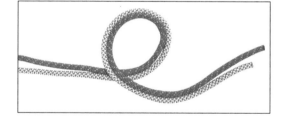

3 Tuck the working ends through the loop.

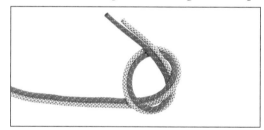

4 Pull tight.

𝄃𝄃𝄃 KNOT NOTES 𝄃𝄃𝄃

The Two Strand Overhand Knot is often used in rappelling applications to tie two ropes together in order to extend the length of the rope. It is known as the European Death Knot because at one time American climbers believed that this knot, which was widely used by European climbers, was the cause of many climbing accidents. This theory has been proven to be untrue, but the name has remained.

HALF HITCH

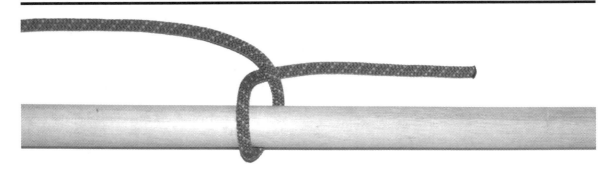

Also known as: *Single Hitch*

The Single Hitch is basically a turn that is secured by its own standing part. It is not typically tied by itself as a knot because of the ease with which it can come undone when used alone; more often, it is used as a part of another knot or doubled (see Two Half Hitches, page 21). The structure of the knot is very basic.

1 Place the working end of the rope around an object.

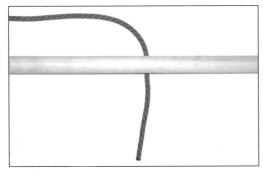

2 Put a turn in the rope, tucking it under its own standing part.

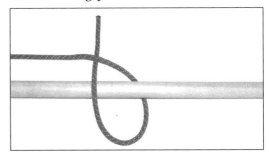

3 Pull tight.

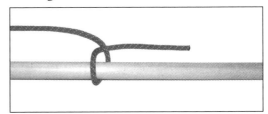

TWO HALF HITCHES

Again relying on the simplicity of the Overhand Knot, Two Half Hitches are the elementary way to tie a rope to an object. If tied correctly, Two Half Hitches will resemble a Clove Hitch (see page 81) around the standing end of the rope.

1 Place the working end of the rope around an object and tie a single Half Hitch.

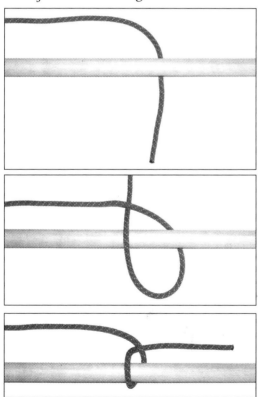

2 Tie a second Half Hitch identical to the first.

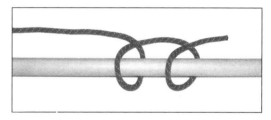

3 Pull tight.

OVERHAND LOOP

This knot is a variation of the Overhand Knot that will give you a loop at the end of your rope. It is often used to secure loads or tie parcels. The advantages of the Overhand Loop are the ease with which it is tied and the fact that you do not need an end of the rope—it can be tied anywhere in the middle. Because it becomes so tight after being cinched down, it is often very difficult or even impossible to untie and must be cut.

1　Place a bight in the rope.

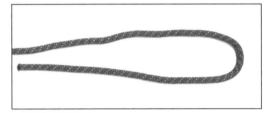

2　Tie an Overhand Knot with the bight.

3　Pull tight.

DOUBLE OVERHAND LOOP

Also known as: *Gut Knot, Surgeon's Loop*

As with the Overhand Loop, the Double Overhand Loop forms a secure and fixed loop at the end of your rope. It is bulky and secure enough that it can be used in smaller, synthetic lines where an Overhand Loop cannot. The Double Overhand Loop is often used in fishing applications and is sometimes modified by passing the bight through the loop a third time. The third wrap does not add much additional strength to the knot, but provides more material, which can make the knot easier to untie.

1 Place a bight in the rope.

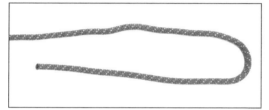

2 Tie an Overhand Knot with the bight.

3 Tuck the bight through the Overhand Knot one more time.

4 Pull tight.

SCAFFOLD KNOT

Also known as: *Overhand Sliding Knot*

The Scaffold Knot is a sliding loop that is easy to tie and cinches down on itself when weighted. The greater the load that is placed on the Scaffold Knot, the tighter it will grip. When tied correctly, it is a strong and secure; when tied incorrectly, it can quickly come undone, creating a dangerous situation.

1 Place a bight in the rope.

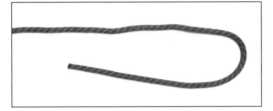

2 With the working end, place a loop around standing end and tuck it through the loop, creating an Overhand Knot.

3 Tuck the running end through the loop twice, creating a Double Overhand Knot.

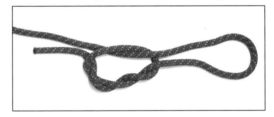

4 Pull tight.

⬤⬤⬤ KNOT NOTES ⬤⬤⬤

The scaffold knot is commonly used by fisherman. It can also be used any time you need to tie a rope around something to secure it or hang something from a high point.

MULTIPLE SCAFFOLD KNOT

The Multiple Scaffold Knot is a slightly stronger version of the Scaffold Knot. The main benefit of the Multiple Scaffold Knot over the Scaffold Knot is visual. There is negligible strength gain, but it is a bulkier knot that offers a feeling of security.

1 Place a bight in the rope.

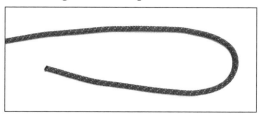

2 With the working end, place a loop around standing end and tuck it through the loop, creating an Overhand Knot.

3 Tuck the running end through the loop three times, creating a Triple Overhand Knot.

4 Pull tight.

OYSTERMAN'S STOPPER KNOT

Also known as: *Ashley's Stopper Knot*

This is a bulkier stopper knot that can be used to prevent the rope from pulling through an object or to prevent an object from sliding off the rope.

1 Place a loop in the rope.

2 Put a bight in the standing end of the rope and tuck it in the underside of the loop.

3 Pull tight, maintaining the bight in the rope.

4 Tuck the running end through the bight.

5 Pull tight.

⫸⫸⫸ KNOT NOTES ⫸⫸⫸

Legend has it that around 1910, Clifford Ashley, author of *The Ashley Book of Knots*, noticed a knot aboard a boat in an oyster fishing fleet. It was lumpy and unrecognizable. What he later determined to be a wet, swollen, and poorly tied Figure Eight Knot had become known as the Oysterman's Stopper Knot or the Ashley's Stopper Knot.

STEVEDORE'S KNOT

The Stevedore's Knot is another in the family of stopper knots. It is more secure than the simple Overhand Knot and can be used in craftwork to prevent beads, for example, from sliding off the cord, or in larger applications such as preventing a rope from pulling through an eyelet or a pulley. It is commonly tied into ropes as a handhold for various purposes, such as a makeshift grip when using rope to traverse difficult terrain.

1 Place a bight in the rope.

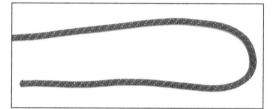

2 Wrap the working end around the standing end two times.

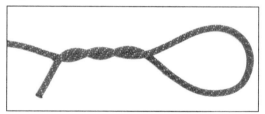

3 Pull the working end up through the bight and pull tight.

*//// KNOT NOTES *

The origin of this knot's name is unclear; one theory is that it was commonly used by stevedores, or dock workers, to prevent their cargo ropes from running through the blocks they used for raising and lowering.

FIGURE EIGHT
STOPPER KNOT

The Figure Eight Stopper Knot, or the "Figure Eight" as it is usually referred to, is a simple stopper knot that is often used by sailors and climbers to prevent rope from pulling through rope bags, pulleys, or the eyelets of sails. It also serves as the basis for several other knots.

1 Place a bight in the rope.

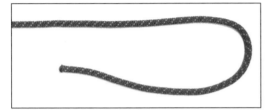

2 Wrap the working end around the standing end one full time.

3 Tuck the working end up through the bight.

4 Pull tight.

〽️ KNOT NOTES 〽️

The figure eight, which is similar to the symbol for infinity, can also be used to represent unending love.

HEAVING LINE KNOT

Also known as: *Monk's Knot, Franciscan Knot*

The Heaving Line Knot is a quick and easy way to add weight to the end of a rope for throwing, such as tossing a line from boat to shore. It also makes a handy, fist-sized grip at the end of a pull rope and is often tied at the end of a decorative rope for its aesthetic appearance. This knot can use a lot of rope, depending on how big you want the knot to be.

1 Place a bight in the working end of the rope.

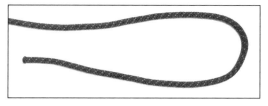

2 Cross the working end over the standing end.

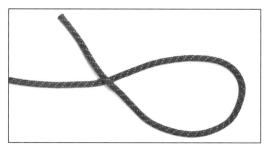

3 Tuck the working end under the standing end and direct it toward the bight.

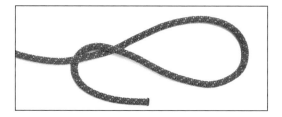

4 Cross the two ends to form a "fish" symbol.

5 Wrap around them working toward the bight.

6 Tuck the working end under the bight and pull the standing end.

7 Pull tight.

Basic Knots 29

MONKEY'S FIST

The Monkey's Fist can be used as a stopper knot, as a rope pull, or as the weighted end of a rope. Initially tying it requires some patience and practice, but once you have the hang of it, it is relatively easy to tie. Sometimes a small spherical object such as a golf ball, wooden bead, or round stone is placed in the middle of the knot for internal support as it approaches completion. Though Monkey's Fists are designed to weight a line, they are often tied as decorative zipper pulls, keychain decor, or even at the end of a lamp or ceiling fan pull cord.

1 Make three complete turns, making sure to hold them flat (right next to each other).

2 Tuck the working end through the center and add three more complete turns perpendicular to the first three turns.

3 Turn the rope 90 degrees again and tuck the working end through the top of the knot between the two sets of turns.

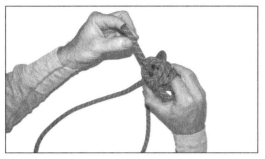

4 Tuck the working end through the bottom of the knot between the two sets of turns.

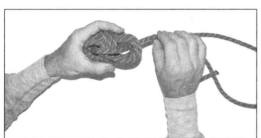

5 Bring the working end up through the top of the knot between the two sets of turns.

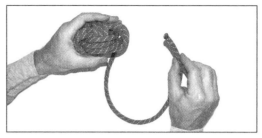

6 Place the rounded object in the middle of the knot (if you wish; this is not always necessary).

7 Progressively tighten the knot a bit at a time, starting with the first turn through the entire knot.

BENDS

Rope bending is the act of joining two ropes together to create a single longer rope. Often used in mountaineering, climbing, and fishing, bends are helpful when a single rope or line won't be adequate to fulfill the function you have in mind.

When a bend is tied, it is typically for a temporary purpose and not for a permanent application, so as a general rule, bends are relatively easy to untie. With smaller diameter cordage such as monofilament, however, you will probably have to cut the line if you want it undone. When tying ropes of differing diameters together, you must take special care to prevent slippage.

There are several bends that rely on symmetry. Two ropes are tied around one another and when the knots are pulled together, they nest perfectly up against one another, which is aesthetically pleasing in addition to providing functional strength.

SHEET BEND

The Sheet Bend is a simple and common way to join two ropes together. It belongs to the family of bends that can be used to tie ropes of differing diameters together. It should be noted that this knot is neither strong nor secure. It is easily undone and reduces the overall strength of the line by over 50 percent. Though this knot has several downsides, it is still worth learning as a quick and easy way to join two ropes for an application that does not involve load bearing or life safety.

1 Place a bight in the first rope.

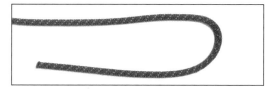

2 Tuck the second rope through the bight.

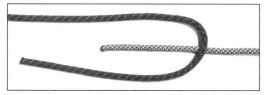

3 Pass the working end of the second rope under the bight of the first.

4 Tuck the working end of the second rope under itself, making sure that the ends of both ropes are on the same side.

5 Pull tight.

💨 KNOT NOTES 💨

The Sheet Bend has a long history in sailing applications. Its name comes from when it was used to attach the sheets (the ropes used to control the sails) to a lower corner of the sail, or *clew*.

FLEMISH BEND

Also known as: *Figure Eight Bend*

This bend, a strong way to join two ropes while maintaining over 80 percent rope strength, is a better option for most situations than the Sheet Bend. It is not as functional with natural fiber ropes due to its propensity to jam, but functions extremely well with more modern, synthetic rope.

1 Make a loop in the first rope.

2 Put a half twist in the loop.

3 Tuck the working end up through the loop, creating a figure eight.

4 Place the working end of the second rope on the standing part of the first rope.

5 Trace the second rope along the first until it also forms a figure eight parallel to the first.

6 Dress the knot so the two strands do not cross each other.

7 Pull tight.

DOUBLE
FIGURE OF EIGHT BEND

The Double Figure of Eight is a simple way to join two knots that looks just as the name would imply. This is a variation of the Flemish Bend. The two figure eights can be kept a few inches apart to leave room for the knots to briefly slide before holding, which can help to absorb a shock. When pulled together, the two figure eights should nest perfectly together.

1 With rope 1, tie a figure eight.

2 Tuck the working end of rope 2 into the loop where the working end of rope 1 resides.

3 Pull through the figure eight in rope 1.

4 With rope 2 tie a figure eight around rope 1.

5 Pull each rope from both ends to tightly secure the knots.

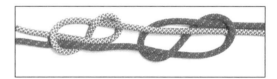

6 Pull the ropes apart to make sure the figure eights will nest properly. If they don't, you probably tied them in two different directions. Try tying the figure eight in rope 2 the opposite direction.

FISHERMAN'S KNOT

Also known as: *Waterman's Knot, Angler's Knot, English Knot, Halibut Knot*

The Fisherman's Knot is two identical overhand knots tied so that when they are drawn together they nest perfectly and the working ends lie in opposing directions. This is a common and secure way to join two ropes or cords of equal diameter together. When it is tied in rope, it can be untied, but in fishing line, it will have to be cut.

1 Tie a simple Overhand Knot in rope 1.

2 Tuck the working end of rope 2 through the Overhand Knot in rope 1.

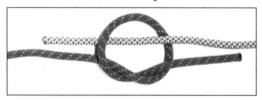

3 In rope 2, tie an Overhand Knot around rope 1.

4 Pull each knot individually to tighten.

5 Pull the ropes apart from each other, drawing the knots in together. If the knots do not nest perfectly, try tying the knot on rope 2 again going the opposite direction.

 **TIP**

To avoid slippage, many choose to tie the Double Fisherman's Knot instead.

DOUBLE FISHERMAN'S KNOT

Also known as: *Grinner Knot, Grapevine Knot, Double Englishman's Knot*

This knot is commonly used in climbing as well as search and rescue. It is a quick and secure way to join ropes of equal diameter. As the name implies, it is similar to a Fisherman's Knot except that the Overhand Knots are doubled.

1 Place the two ropes parallel to one another.

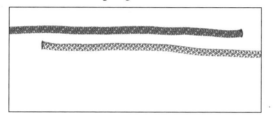

2 Make a loop in rope 1 around rope 2.

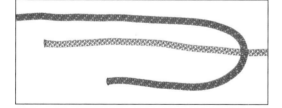

3 Create a figure eight working back toward its own standing end, making sure you finish it by tucking the working end under both ropes 1 and 2.

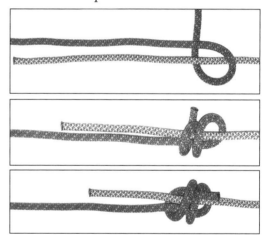

4 Pull both ends of rope 1 to secure it to rope 2.

5 With the working end of rope 2 repeat Step 3, tying it around rope 1.

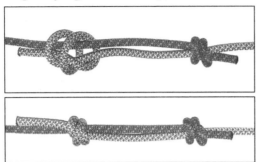

6 Pull the ropes apart, drawing the knots in together.

 **TIP**

A third wrap can be added to form a Triple Fisherman's Knot if slippage is a concern with the Double Fisherman's Knot.

ZEPPELIN BEND

Also known as: *Rosendahl Bend*

The Zeppelin Bend is capable of joining anything from the thickest of ropes to the smallest. Although slightly unsightly, it is possibly the most trustworthy of all the bend knots. The trick to the Zeppelin Bend is correctly tucking the running ends through the loop.

1 Place an overhand loop in rope 1.

2 Place an underhand loop in rope 2.

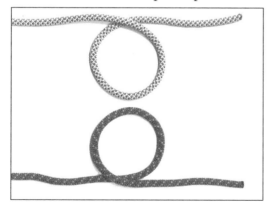

3 Place the loop in rope 1 on top of the loop in rope 2.

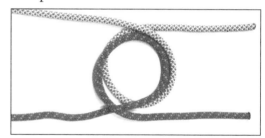

4 Tuck the running end of each loop over its own running end and thread through the loops.

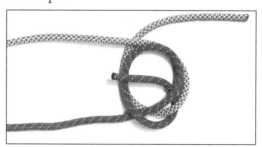

5 Pull the ends of each individual rope tightly to secure the knots.

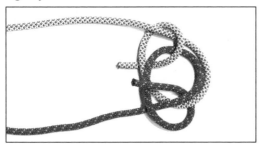

6 Pull the two ropes apart from each other.

//// KNOT NOTES ////

This knot originated in the 1930s when naval officer Charles Rosendahl required his men to use this bend when mooring lighter-than-air ships.

ADJUSTABLE BEND

The Adjustable Bend Knot is a slide-and-grip knot that will slide along the rope and absorb the energy created by the momentum of a fall. The knots will slide along the rope as they grip tighter until they are coupled.

1 Place the ropes parallel to one another.

2 Place a bight in rope 1 and wrap it a minimum of three times around rope 2.

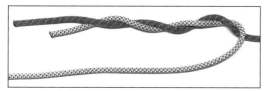

3 Pass the working end of rope 1 around and beneath the wrapped rope (rope 2) and its own standing part.

4 Tuck the working end under its own final turn.

5 Work the ends of the knot until it is secure around rope 2.

6 Repeat steps 1–5 to tie rope 2 around rope 1.

◢◢◢ KNOT NOTES ◣◣◣

This bend was designed by Canadian climber Robert Chisnall around 1982. It can be tied in rope or webbing. Tests on this knot show that a fourth wrap can increase the knot strength by anywhere from 10 percent to over 25 percent, depending on the diameter rope used.*

*(Source: *The Complete Book of Knots* by Geoffrey Budworth, p. 95)

HARNESS BEND

The Harness Bend is useful when joining two ropes that must remain under tension, such as when there is a load on both ropes. It is often used for tying parcels. Its main benefit is the fact that it can be tied from a wide variety of materials including leather and fence wire.

1 Place the two ropes parallel to each other.

2 Tuck rope 1 under rope 2 and then back over it.

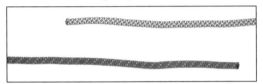

3 Bring the working end of rope 1 back under its own standing end.

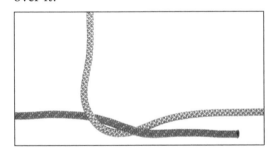

4 Pass the working end of rope 2 around the standing end of rope 1.

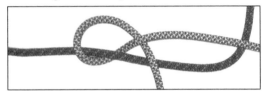

5 Tuck it under itself, creating a half hitch.

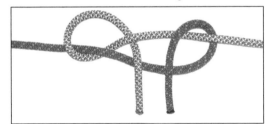

6 Pull tight.

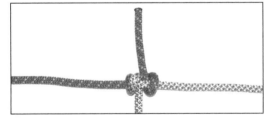

///// KNOT NOTES \\\\\

The name Harness Bend comes from the origins of the knot, which lie in its use in the days of horse-drawn carriages by carters (someone who transports a load by way of cart) and wagoneers.

DOUBLE HARNESS BEND
WITH PARALLEL ENDS

Many people who tie knots prefer symmetrical knots due to the fact that they are more pleasing to the eye and can be easier to learn and memorize. The Double Harness Bend with Parallel Ends is often preferred over the Harness Bend for just those reasons.

1 Place the two ropes parallel to one another.

2 Tuck the working end of rope 1 beneath rope 2.

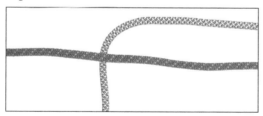

3 Bring the working end back up and under its own standing part.

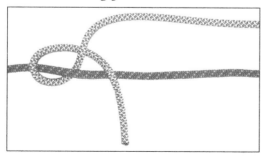

4 Repeat steps 2 and 3 as you tie rope 2 around rope 1.

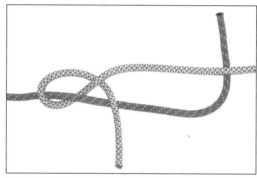

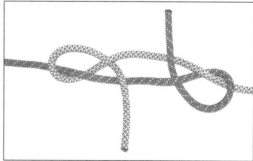

5 Pull the individual knots tight.

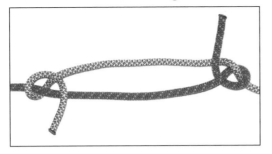

6 Pull the standing ends apart from each other, bringing the knots together.

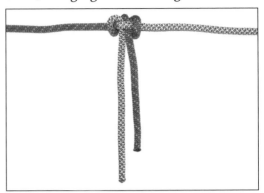

SURGEON'S KNOT

This is a common way to join two ropes of similar diameter, used in fishing to tie a leader onto the end of the line and in craftwork to join two small cords together. Most often seen in smaller diameter nylon and monofilament and in natural-fiber ropes, the Surgeon's Knot can be tied in all types and sizes of rope. There are several variations of this knot depending on its intended use.

1   Cross the working ends of ropes 1 and 2.

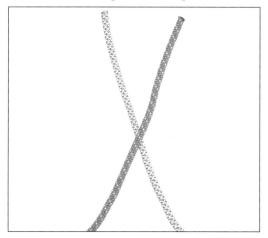

2   Wrap the working end of either rope around the other rope two times, making note of the direction you went around.

3   Bring the working ends together again and tuck one working end under the other going in the opposite direction of the first wraps.

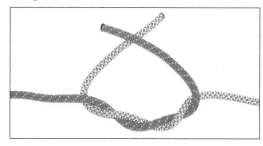

4   To tighten, pull each working end and its adjacent standing end.

5   Pull the standing ends apart, allowing the knot to twist slightly so that it lays diagonally.

HUNTER'S BEND

Also known as: *Rigger's Bend*

Like the Zeppelin Bend, the Hunter's Bend is one of very few knots "invented" in this century. It is formed by tying two intertwined overhand knots and is a stable knot that can be tied in a variety of cords. One of the things that makes the Hunter's Bend popular is that is easy to untie.

1 Create a loop in rope 1.

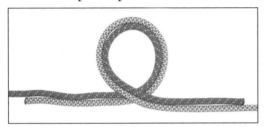

2 Tuck rope 2 into the loop of rope 1 and create a loop by bringing the working end under the pair of loops.

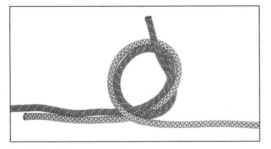

3 Tuck the working end of the front rope in the back and through the loops.

4 Tuck the working end of the back rope in the front and through the loops.

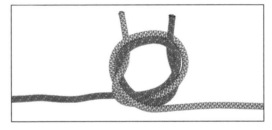

5 Pull the ropes tight while maintaining the integrity of the knot.

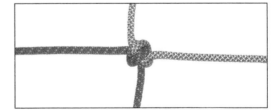

///// KNOT NOTES \\\\\

The Rigger's Bend was created by American Phil Smith during World War II, but it did not become well known until 1978, when Dr. E. Hunter rediscovered it. The attention he received for the knot led to the formation of the International Guild of Knot Tyers in 1982.

STROP BEND

The Strop Bend is a simple way to tie two loops together. It is often used in craftwork, but is strong enough to endure the rigors of hard labor. It can be tied in virtually any type of cord. The appearance of a Strop Bend is similar to that of a Square (Reef) Knot but the dynamics differ in that a Strop Bend joins two loops. Similarly, though, the Strop Bend can only come untied if one of the ropes breaks.

1 Tuck a bight of rope 1 into the bight of rope 2.

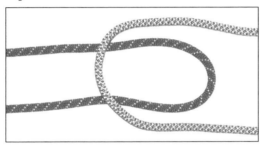

2 Double the working end of the bight you just tucked back onto itself.

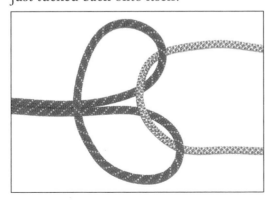

3 Draw the standing part of rope 1 through the secondary loop.

4 Pull tight.

VICE VERSA

The Vice Versa is a tight bend that is most commonly tied in wet cordage, where other bends will slip. It has a very distinctive look when finished.

1 Lay the two ropes parallel to one another.

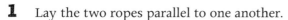

2 Tuck the working end of rope 1 under rope 2.

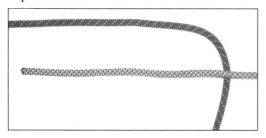

3 Pass the end over rope 2 and then beneath itself.

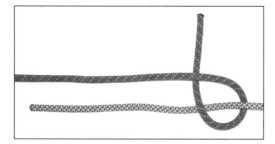

4 Tuck the working end of rope 2 under rope 1.

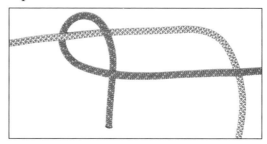

5 Pass the end over rope 2 and the beneath itself.

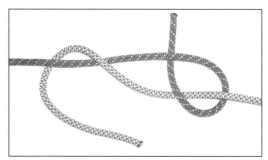

6 Cross the right end over the left end.

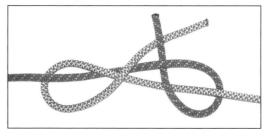

7 Tuck it through the left loop.

8 Tuck the remaining end through the right loop.

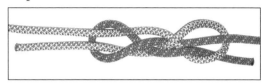

9 Pull tight.

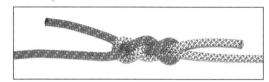

░░░ KNOT NOTES ░░░

As with many other knots, the origin of the Vice Versa is debated. Scientist Harry Asher "discovered" this knot and published it in his book *The Alternative Knot Book* in 1989. An earlier version was created by writer and traveler Tim Severin in 1978 to hold together leather thongs in a cow-hide boat he made.

SIMPLE SIMON OVER

The Simple Simon Over is a simple knot that is surprisingly not that common. It is a variation of a Square Knot. Rarely found in books, it is extremely effective in tying wet, synthetic rope together.

1   Make a bight in rope 1.

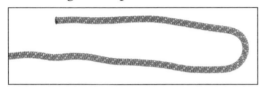

2   Tuck the working end of rope 2 through the bight in rope 1.

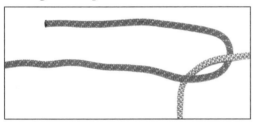

3   Wrap the working end of rope 2 over both the working and standing ends of rope 1.

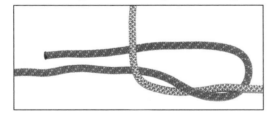

4   Continue wrapping over the working and standing ends of rope 1.

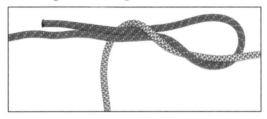

5   Crossing the working end over itself, tuck it back into the back of the bight in rope 1.

6   Pull tight.

⁄⁄⁄ TIP ⁄⁄⁄

Tie it so that the working ends are on the same side of the knot. Otherwise the knot is apt to pull through and come undone. If your working ends turn up on opposite sides of the knot, simply try again, this time wrapping the working end of rope 2 the other way around rope 1.

SIMPLE SIMON UNDER

A variation of the Simple Simon Over, the Simple Simon Under actually creates a more secure knot by changing a single step (the first part of step 5). It has the added attribute of being able to connect two ropes of unequal diameter.

1 Make a bight in rope 1.

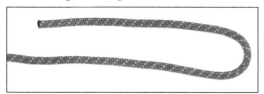

2 Tuck the working end of rope 2 through the bight in rope 1.

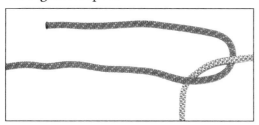

3 Wrap the working end of rope 2 over both the working and standing ends of rope 1.

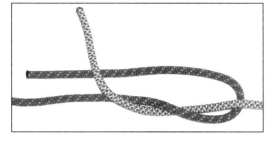

4 Continue wrapping over the working and standing ends of rope 1.

5 Crossing the working end under itself, tuck it back into the back of the bight in rope 1.

6 Pull tight.

〰️ KNOT NOTES 〰️

The Simple Simon Knots were first published by Harry Asher in 1989.

SIMPLE SIMON DOUBLE

This variation of the Harry Asher Simple Simon knots is actually the strongest of them. The Simple Simon Double is effective in tying two ropes of different diameters and textures together and has become extremely popular for use in fishing..

1 Make a bight in rope 1.

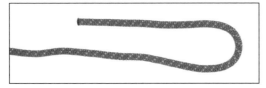

2 Tuck the working end of rope 2 through the bight in rope 1.

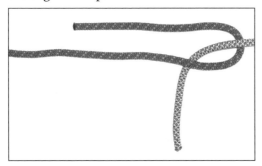

3 Wrap the working end of rope 2 around both the working and standing ends of rope 1 and then over them both.

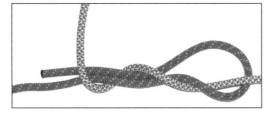

4 Wrap the working end of rope 2 around a second time.

5 Crossing the working end over itself, tuck it back into the back of the bight in rope 1.

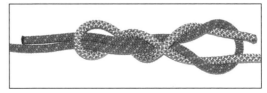

6 Pull tight.

BOWLINE BEND

The advantage to the Bowline Bend is that it can be used to tie virtually any two kinds of cordage together. The Bowline is a strong, time-tested, reliable knot. The only weakness in this bend is where the two loops interlock and rub against one another.

1 Make a loop in rope 1 with enough working end to create the size of bight you are going to want in your finished knot. (You may not know what size bight you want. It's perfectly OK to tie the knot, determine how big you want the bight, and then retie, adjusting as necessary.)

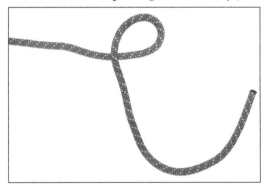

2 Pass the working end up through the loop, around the standing end, and then back down through the loop.

3 Holding the bight and the working end, pull tight.

4 Make a loop in rope 2 with enough working end to create the size of bight you are going to want in your finished knot.

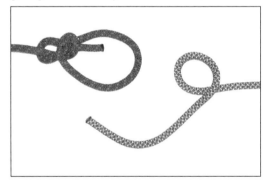

5 Tuck the working end of rope 2 through the bowline in rope 1.

6 Pass the working end up through the loop, around the standing end, and then back down through the loop.

7 Holding the bight and working end of rope 2, pull tight.

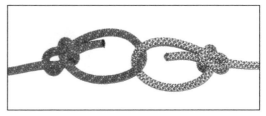

TWIN BOWLINE BEND

The Twin Bowline Bend has the advantage of utilizing strong and popular bowlines, but without the liability found in the Bowline Bend of the two loops rubbing against each other causing potential failure. When the Twin Bowline Bend is placed under a load, the knots share equal amounts of strain and cinch down on the standing parts of the other rope, which is useful when you need to extend the length of your rope but want as much strength as possible.

1 Place the working end of the ropes parallel to one another.

2 Form a loop in the standing part of rope 1.

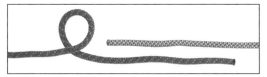

3 Tuck rope 2 through the loop in rope 1.

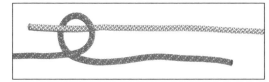

4 Pass it around the standing part of rope 1 and back through the loop.

5 Pull tight.

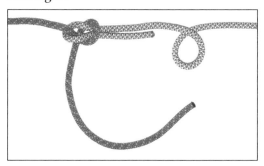

6 Flip the knot around and repeat steps 1–5, beginning by placing a loop in the standing part of rope 2.

7 Pull on the working ends to tighten.

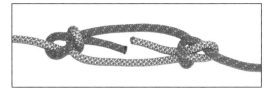

SHAKE HANDS

Another knot designed by Harry Asher, the Shake Hands is an easy-to-tie and secure way to join two ropes. It is effective in joining equal-diameter rope of nearly any material.

1   Make an overhand loop in rope 1.

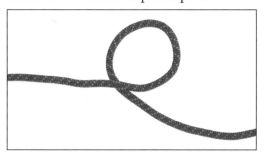

2   Tuck rope 2 through the loop in rope 1 and make an underhand loop.

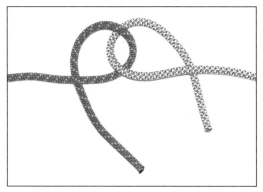

3   Take the working end of rope 1 under the loops and tuck it through the common space between the two ropes in the middle of the knot.

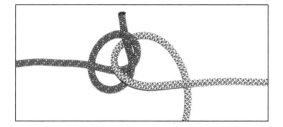

4   Tuck the working end of rope 2 down through the common space between the two ropes. At this point the knot should look like a pretzel.

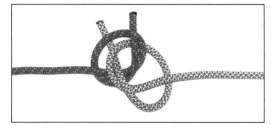

5   Pull on the working ends to tighten.

ALPINE BUTTERFLY BEND

The Alpine Butterfly Bend is based on the Alpine Butterfly (see page 129). While this is a secure way to tie two ropes together, caution should be taken. Incorrect tying can result in a knot that is similar in appearance, but far less secure.

1 Make an underhand loop in rope 1.

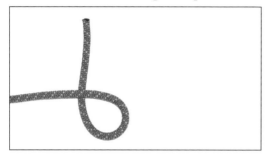

2 Tuck rope 2 through the loop in rope 1 and make an underhand loop.

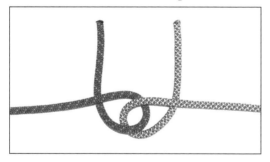

3 Tuck both working ends down through the common space in the middle of the knot.

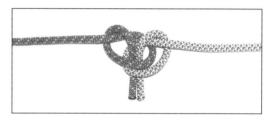

4 Pull tight.

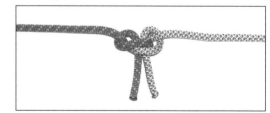

BLOOD KNOT

The Blood Knot enables you to join two cords together while maintaining the majority of their strength, making it a favorite among fishermen, who use it to join two monofilament lines together. It can also be used in equal diameter rope of any size that will allow you to tie the knot.

1 Place the working ends of two ropes together.

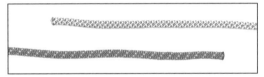

2 Begin wrapping rope 1 around both ropes, working back toward its standing end.

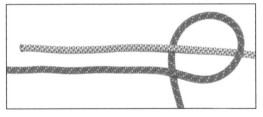

3 You should complete a minimum of five turns.

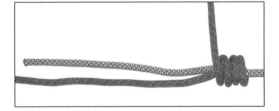

4 Tuck the working end between the two ropes and trap it there while you complete the knot.

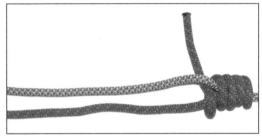

5 Begin wrapping rope 2 around both ropes, working back toward its standing end.

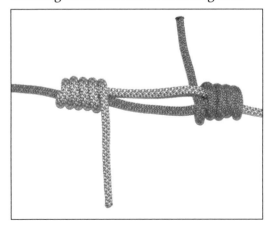

6 After wrapping the same number of times (minimum of five) that you did with rope 1, tuck the working end between the ropes in the opposite direction from rope 1.

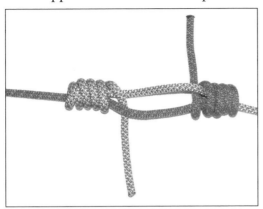

7 Tighten the knot by pulling the standing ends and cinching down the wraps.

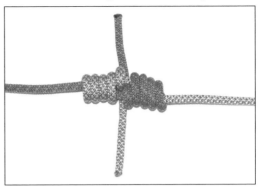

⫸ TIP ⫷

Fishermen recommend moistening the lines with saliva or water to make them more supple when tying the Blood Knot.

DOUBLE GRINNER KNOT

Also known as: *Paragum Knot*

Also popular in fishing, the Double Grinner Knot is a common way to tie two lines of equal diameter together. There is some debate among anglers whether or not to use the knot with braided lines. Most would agree that if you tie the Double Grinner Knot with a braided fishing line, you should increase your number of wraps.

1 Lay the working ends of your two ropes parallel to one another.

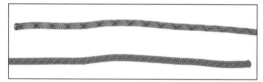

2 Place rope 1 in a bight over rope 2.

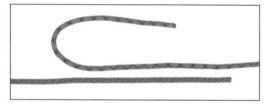

3 Tuck the working end of rope 1 under rope 2 and its own standing end.

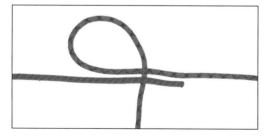

4 Wrap the working end of rope 1 around both ropes two times, working back toward its own standing end.

5 Tuck the working end under its own two loops and away from the standing end. Pull rope 1 tight.

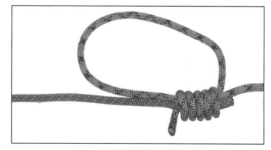

6 Repeat steps 2–5, wrapping rope 2 around rope 1.

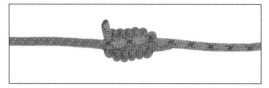

7 Pull rope 2 tight.

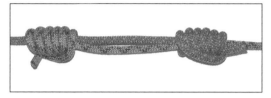

8 Pull the standing ends away from one another until the two knots meet.

///// **TIP** \\\\\

When tying the Double Grinner Knot in a monofilament fishing line, you may want to use a pair of pliers to tighten each of the two knots within the Double Grinner Knot in order to make sure it is seated completely.

BINDING KNOTS

Knots that use both ends of the rope to keep an object or multiple objects tied together are called "binding knots." Bindings are the knots you see used to wrap parcels or tied around boat docks to lash posts to the structure. There are two types of binding knots: those that are held together by friction and those that are held together by the ends being tied. Friction-based binding knots are commonly used to tie around the end of a rope to keep it from fraying.

Binding knots should only be used for the aforementioned purposes, not as a hitch (which ties a rope to an object) or a bend (which joins two ropes together).

GRANNY KNOT

Other than being one of the most common knots that can be tied, there is little good that can be said about the Granny Knot. It is mentioned here mostly so that you will recognize it and thus be able to avoid it. It should never be used under a load or in any type of life safety situation. It looks deceptively like a Square Knot (see page 65), but is even less trustworthy than the already inferior Square Knot. The key visual difference is the lack of symmetry in the Granny Knot.

1 Cross the two ends of the same rope, one over the other, in this case left over right.

2 Tie a Half Knot. Note that the two ropes are intertwined counterclockwise.

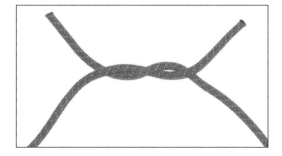

3 Bring the two ends together again, crossing the same way (again, in this case, left over right).

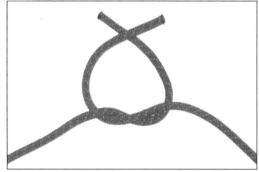

4 Tie another Half Knot.

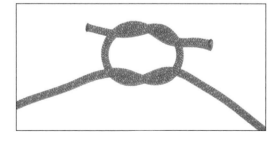

5 Pull tight.

▰▰▰ **TIP** ▰▰▰

The Granny Knot is commonly used to tie shoes (don't let the loops throw you off). If your shoes often come untied, you may be tying a Granny Knot, rather than a Square (or Reef) Knot. This can be corrected by simply wrapping the second loop the other direction around the first. See page 65 to learn how to tie the Square Knot.

SQUARE KNOT

Also known as: *Reef Knot*

This knot has been incorrectly taught for decades. It is often recommended for use as a bend (tying two ropes together), despite the fact that it easily and dangerously comes apart under a load. It is attractive, symmetrical, and easy to tie, but also weak and subject to slippage. It should never be used where a heavy load or a life is at stake, but only be as a binding. In *The Ashley Book of Knots,* Clifford Ashley says, "There have probably been more lives lost as a result of using a square knot as a bend (tying two ropes together) than from the failure of any other half dozen knots combined."

1 Bring together the two ends of the same rope.

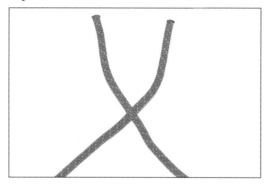

2 Cross them left over right and tuck the left under the right, creating a Half Knot.

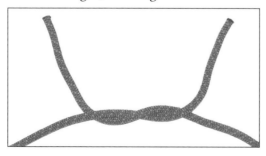

3 Now bring the two ends back together.

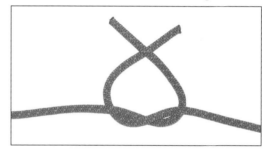

4 Cross them right over left and tuck the right one under, finishing the knot.

5 Pull tight. The working ends should be on the same side of the knot. If they are on opposite ends you have a Thief Knot (see page 67).

**///// TIP **

The Square Knot is generally taught as "left over right, right over left." But if it is more natural for you, the knot can also be tied the opposite way (right over left, left over right).

THIEF KNOT

The Thief Knot looks very similar to a Square Knot. The only difference is that the working ends end up on opposite sides of the knot, rather than on the same side. The Thief Knot is, for all intents and purposes, useless. It is included in this book only to demonstrate the difference between it and a Square Knot so you don't make the mistake of thinking you tied the Square Knot when you've actually tied a weaker version of that already weak knot.

1 Place a bight in one end of the rope.

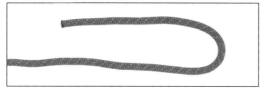

2 Tuck the other end through the bight toward the short end and wrap it around both parts of the bight.

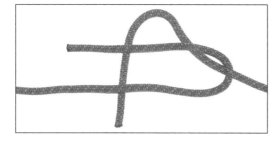

3 Lead the working end back through the bight.

4 Pull tight.

◢◢◢ KNOT NOTES ◣◣◣

Although there isn't much evidence regarding the origin of the Thief Knot, a common theory is that it was used to determine if someone has been in your bag or kit. If you secure your bag or kit with a Thief Knot, a "thief" may, at quick glance, assume it is a Square Knot. After they have gone through your things, they will re-secure your bag or kit with a Square Knot, leaving you clear evidence that someone has been in there.

CONSTRICTOR KNOT

This is probably the most commonly tied, useful, and functional of the binding knots. The Constrictor Knot can be used for a variety of things such as a temporary whipping at the end of a rope to keep it from coming unraveled, a clamp to hold things down, or a grip around a group of objects. This knot should be added to your arsenal of knots that you know by heart.

1 Wrap the cord around whatever is to be tied.

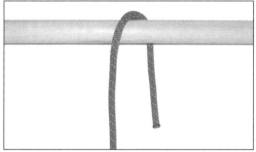

2 Lay the working end across its own standing part.

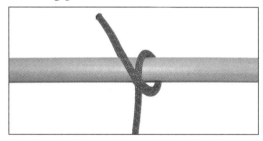

3 Tuck the working around the object again, creating an "X."

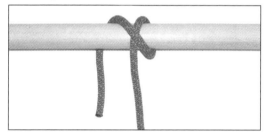

4 Lead the working end beneath the diagonal part of the "X" that was just created.

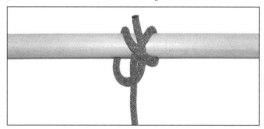

5 Tuck the working end under the first crossing turn that you made.

6 Pull tight.

 **TIP**

The Constrictor Knot is tied the same way as a Clove Hitch (see page 81), with the tucked working end added for additional security.

DOUBLE CONSTRICTOR KNOT

When a Constrictor Knot would be appropriate but you require or would feel more comfortable with added strength, a Double Constrictor Knot is a good option. It is particularly useful when tying cords that are slippery or tend to pull through.

1 Wrap the cord around whatever is to be tied.

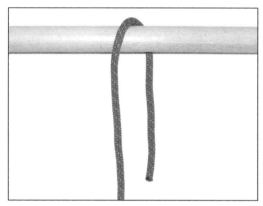

2 Lay the working end across its own standing part.

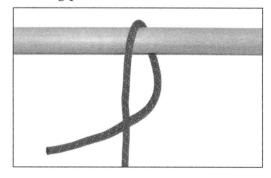

3 Tuck the working end around the object again, creating an "X."

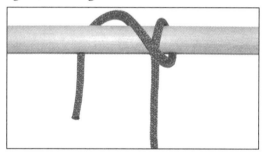

4 Go around the object one more time.

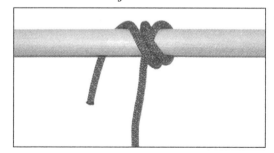

5 Lead the working end beneath the two diagonal parts of the "X" that was just created.

6 Tuck the working end under the first crossing turn that you made.

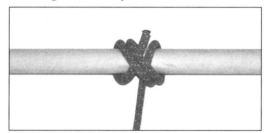

7 Pull tight.

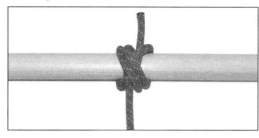

TRANSOM KNOT

This knot was designed to hold two sticks together at right angles to each other. The common belief is that knot pioneer Clifford Ashley created this knot to lash together two cross sticks for his daughter's kite. It has a wide range of uses, particularly in outdoors scenarios (for example, fastening poles together for a tent or other shelter).

1 Place the items to be tied together at a right angle to one another, creating a "cross."

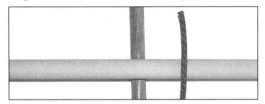

2 Wrap the working end of the rope around the vertical part above the uppermost horizontal part of the "cross." The working end should be diagonal to its own standing end.

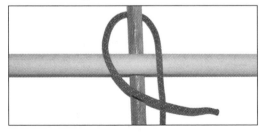

3 Wrap the working end around the vertical part below the horizontal part (in the same direction you previously wrapped above the horizontal part).

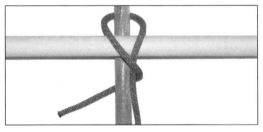

4 Tuck the working end toward the top under both turns.

**///) TIP **

To reinforce the Transom Knot, rotate the "cross" 90 degrees and tie another knot perpendicular to the first.

BAG KNOT

Also known as: *Sack Knot, Miller's Knot*

As the name would imply, the Bag Knot dates back to a time when sacks of granular and powdered materials were placed into bags that were tied at the top to secure them for storage and transport.

1 With the working end of the rope, place a turn around the bag.

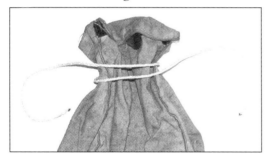

2 Cross the working end under the turn.

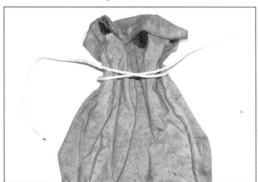

3 Make a second turn around the bag.

4 Bring the working end over the standing end and tuck the working end under both turns.

5 Pull tight.

PACKER'S KNOT

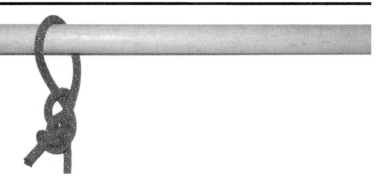

When you need to pull a rope taut around an object, the Packer's Knot is an easy and common way to do it. Once the rope is tied around the object, the standing end can be pulled to tighten the knot and hold it in place.

1 Wrap the working end of the rope around an object.

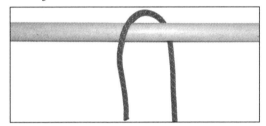

2 Tie a Figure Eight Knot around the standing end of the rope.

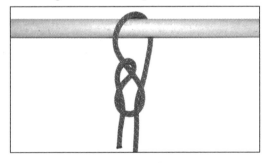

3 With the remaining standing end, tie an Overhand Knot as a safety.

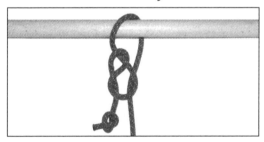

4 Pull tight.

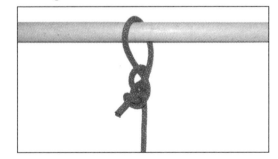

///// KNOT NOTES \\\\\

A similar knot called the Butcher's Knot is tied the exact same way, except with an Overhand Knot instead of a Figure Eight. It serves the same purpose, but is not as strong as the Packer's Knot.

BOA KNOT

The Boa Knot is a binding knot best used to constrict around a cylindrical object. This knot is symmetrical, easy to tie, and very strong.

1 Make a loop (could be an overhand or underhand loop) in the rope.

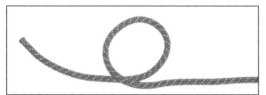

2 Add a second loop identical to the first on top of the first one.

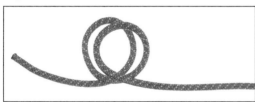

3 Arrange the loops in a coil, making sure both ends are facing the same direction.

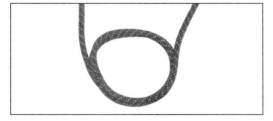

4 Rotate the right side of the coil 180 degrees. It should be in the form of an "8" now, with the right end and left end facing opposite directions.

5 Insert the object that you wish to lash through the first loop and then the second.

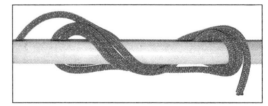

6 Dress the knot and pull tight.

🪢 KNOT NOTES 🪢

One of the more modern knots, the Boa Knot was "discovered" in 1996 by Peter Collingwood. His goal was to design a knot that would remain in place when the object around which it is tied was cut or broken close to the knot.

BOTTLE SLING KNOT

When you look at the steps, this knot may seem daunting, and the first few times you attempt to tie it may be awkward. Despite the numerous steps, however, the Bottle Sling is an easy-to-tie knot with many practical uses, such as creating a handle for a jug or bottle of water, gasoline, etc.

1 Locate the middle of the piece of cord you are intending to use. (The length of cord will depend on how long of a sling you want to create. You should tie this several times to determine what length rope will create what length of sling.) Make a bight at the midpoint.

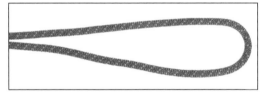

2 Fold the bight down to create two identical loops.

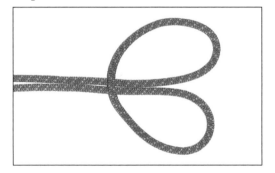

3 Overlap the two loops.

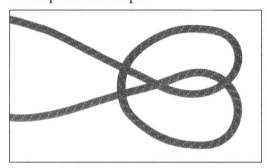

4 Tuck the lower section of the cord, which overlays both legs of the original bight, up through the left loop.

5 Tuck that same part though the central shared space between the two loops and out the right side.

6 Fold the large loop on the back of the knot down to the two legs (standing parts).

7 There will be a similar large loop on the front of the knot. Fold it down to match the part you folded down in step 6.

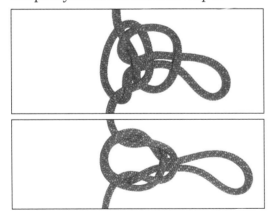

8 Place the area that you've created as the sling over a bottle or jug. Pull both ends of the knot.

9 You can then tie the two standing ends through the bight with a Double Fisherman's Knot (or any other preferred bend) to create the handle.

/// KNOT NOTES **

This fun and easy-to-tie knot likely dates back to ancient times, when people needed to carry water jugs over great distances. It has also been used by cowboys to create makeshift bridles for their horses.

ASHER'S EQUALIZER

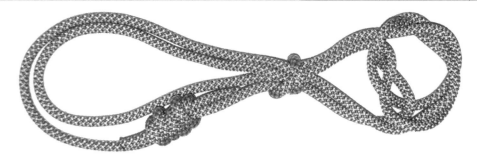

Some consider this knot an upgrade to the Bottle Sling Knot. It is a fun and clever knot that automatically adjusts loop lengths to give you two handles of the same size.

1 Tie a Bottle Sling Knot (see page 76).

2 On one end of the knot you will have a bight and on the other you will have the two rope ends. Tie those ends together with a Double Fisherman's Knot (page 37).

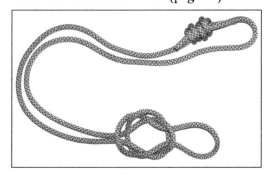

3 Tuck the two sides of the larger loop into the smaller bight on the opposite side of the knot. Do not tuck it all the way in.

4 Feed the end of the loop over the two parts of the rope that you've pulled partway through.

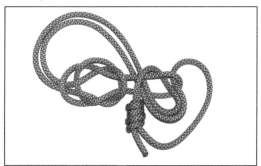

5 Pull the two parts and tighten the knot,
giving you two handles of equal length.

◢◢◢ KNOT NOTES ◣◣◣

Asher's Equalizer was devised in the mid-1980s by Dr. Harry Asher.

MARLINE HITCH

Like many other knots, the Marline Hitch serves multiple purposes. As its name implies, it has the characteristics of a hitch, but it also is commonly used as a binding knot. It is most often used to fasten an object that has been secured by another knot.

1 Tie a knot to secure a rope to the object (pictured here: a Clove Hitch).

2 Pull that knot tight and tie a Half Hitch around the object.

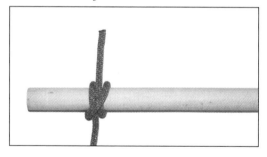

3 Pull the first Half Hitch tight and, a short distance up the object, tie another Half Hitch.

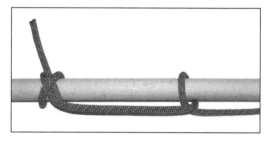

4 Continue tying Half Hitches up the object until it is secure.

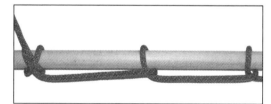

CLOVE HITCH

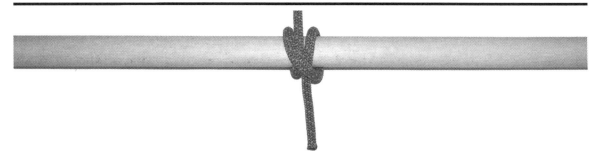

This is one of the most commonly used hitches because it is simple and, as long as it remains taut, strong. It can easily slip, though, if the knot loosens. The best way to prevent this is by holding tension on the rope until the hitch becomes tight. The Clove Hitch can be tied on its own and then slipped over an object, or it can be tied around the object.

1 Pass the working end of the rope around the object to which you are tying. Pull enough rope to wrap it again.

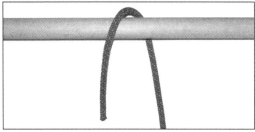

2 While holding the part of the rope that just passed around the object, cross the working end over the standing end.

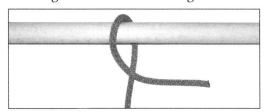

3 Wrap the working end around the object again, going in the same direction as the first loop.

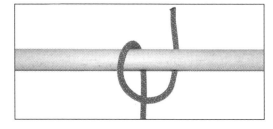

4 Tuck the working end under the part that crossed the working end.

5 Pull tight.

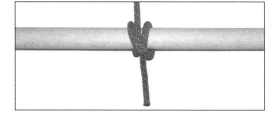

✍✍ TIP ✍✍

You can add safety to the Clove Hitch by continuing the Working End around the object and tying an Overhand Knot to the Working End (see page 82).

CLOVE HITCH WITH A WORKING END

The Clove Hitch with a Working End has a few benefits not offered by the traditional Clove Hitch. With the working end you can add a draw loop that will allow you to use the loop for whatever function you need and to also easily pull the draw loop back through, effectively undoing the knot. This version of the Clove Hitch cannot be tied out in the open; it must be tied around an object.

1 Pass the working end of the rope around the object to which you are tying. Pull enough rope to wrap it again.

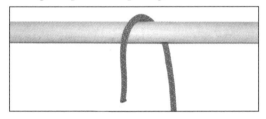

2 While holding the part of the rope that just passed around the object, cross the working end over the standing end.

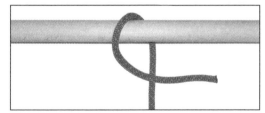

3 Wrap the working end around the object again, going in the same direction as the first loop.

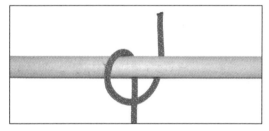

4 Instead of tucking the working end under the cross part of the rope as you did with the Clove Hitch, put a bight in the working end and tuck it under the cross part of the rope.

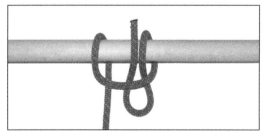

5 Pull the working end and the part of the draw loop coming out of the hitch to tighten.

FIGURE OF EIGHT HITCH

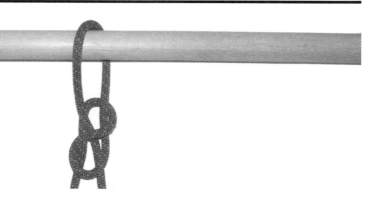

Lacking the strength of other hitches, the Figure of Eight it is easy to tie and functional in jobs that will demand little from it. It is also easily untied, which is an asset in light work situations, but can be dangerous in others. This hitch can be used to temporarily tie something that isn't a heavy load, such as attaching a pet leash to a tree or a kayak to a dock.

1 Pass the working end of the rope around an object (this shown front to back in the illustration).

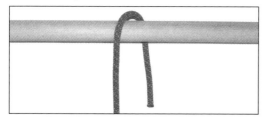

2 Tie a Figure of Eight by wrapping the working end around the standing end one complete time.

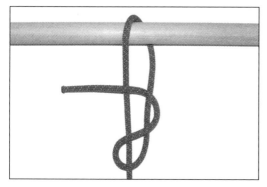

3 Tuck the working end back up through the loop, completing the Figure of Eight.

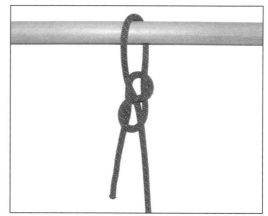

PEDIGREE COW HITCH

A useful and easily tied all-purpose hitch, the Pedigree Cow Hitch is a strong and stable hitch when the load is at a 90-degree angle from the point of attachment. When the load is at a shorter angle, though, it becomes unstable and can slip. In those situations, other hitches such as the Clove Hitch or Rolling Hitch should be used.

1 Wrap the working end of the rope around an object (this is shown front to back in the illustration).

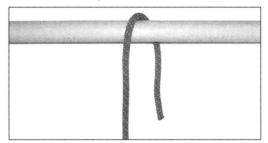

2 Cross the working end around its own standing part.

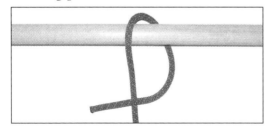

3 Wrap the end back around the object, going from under it to over it.

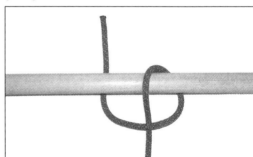

4 Tuck the working end under the bight at the front of the knot.

5 Lead the working end through the two loops to secure it.

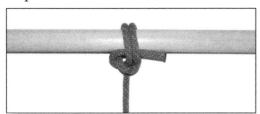

6 Pull tight.

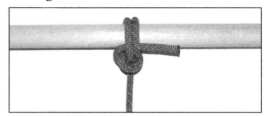

⚓ KNOT NOTES ⚓

This version of the Cow Hitch knot was first published in Harry Asher's book *The Alternative Knot Book* in 1989.

COW HITCH VARIANT

Also known as: *Piwich Knot*

An even stronger and more secure version of the Pedigree Cow Hitch is the Cow Hitch Variant. This knot is commonly used a sturdy hitch in rope applications, but is also often used in craftwork and jewelry making.

1 Wrap the working end of the rope around an object.

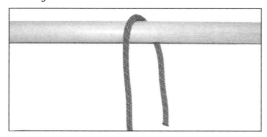

2 Make a Half Hitch around the standing part of the rope.

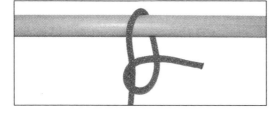

3 Pass the working end around the front of the knot and wrap the working end of the rope again around the object.

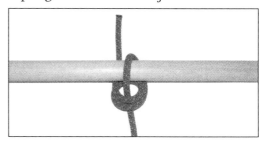

4 Tuck the working end through the turns next to the standing part of the rope.

5 Pull tight.

////// KNOT NOTES \\\\\\

This variant was first published in 1995 by Robert Pont, who named it the Piwich Knot after the boy (Piwich Kust) who tied it.

BUNTLINE HITCH

Also known as: *Stunsail Tack Bend, Studding Sail Tack Bend, Inside Clove Hitch*

This hitch is basically two Half Hitches and is used in situations where the rope is subject to a lot of motion, such as a flag halyard. It is simple and effective. The fact that its use in sailing applications has been documented for centuries is a testament to its reliability.

1 Pass the working end around an object or through its anchor point.

2 Take the working end one full turn around the standing end.

3 Pass the working end across the loop that has been formed.

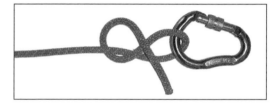

4 Place the working end into the loop from the back of the knot.

5 Pull tight.

〰️ KNOT NOTES 〰️

Buntlines are used to lift the middle portion of a large sail. Typically, there are four to eight buntlines across a sail and they are secured with a Buntline Hitch.

GROUND LINE HITCH

The Ground Line Hitch is an effective way to tie a rope to an object, or more commonly, a smaller cord to a larger cord. It is similar to the popular Clove Hitch, but has proven to be more secure.

1 Pass the working end over the top of the object you are tying around.

2 Cross over (pictured left to right) the standing part.

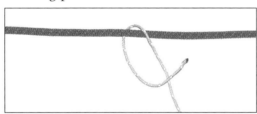

3 Run the working end over the top again.

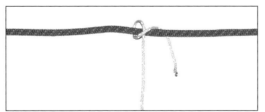

4 Pull the standing part up to create a bight.

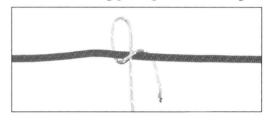

5 Tuck the working end through the bight created in Step 4.

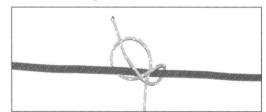

6 Pull tight.

**///// KNOT NOTES **

The Ground Line Hitch was so named because it is used to attach a net to a "ground line," which is the weighted rope at the bottom of a net.

ANCHOR BEND

Also known as: *Fisherman's Bend*

This knot is used to attach a rope to a ring or similar termination point. It is easily tied and, even after being subjected to moderate loads, can be untied. It has been known to jam in modern, synthetic ropes, but is still commonly used for many applications, including the one that gave it its name—tying a cord to an anchor rode.

1 Pass the working end of the rope around an object from the front, going over the top.

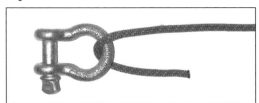

2 Bring the working end around a second time, creating a round turn.

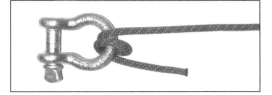

3 Cross the working end over the standing part.

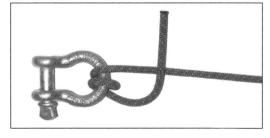

4 Tuck the working end through the round turn.

5 Tie a half hitch around the standing part of the line.

6 Pull tight.

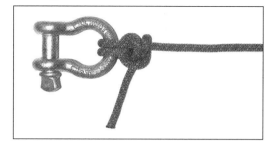

///// **KNOT NOTES** \\\\\

The Anchor Bend has a misleading name, as it is actually a hitch. It was named at a time when the term "bend" was used to mean "to tie to."

ANCHOR BEND VARIANT

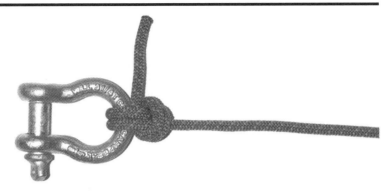

This variation of the Anchor Bend dates back to the early 1900s. It is an easy-to-tie and secure way to attach a rope to an anchor point.

1 Pass the working end of the rope around an object from the front, going over the top.

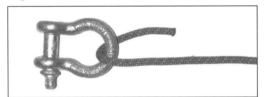

2 Bring the working end around a second time, creating a round turn.

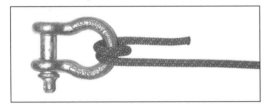

3 Cross the working end over the standing part.

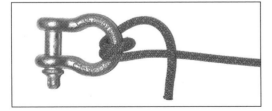

4 Tuck the working end through the round turn.

5 Tuck the working end through a second turn, effectively creating a round turn within a round turn.

6 Pull tight.

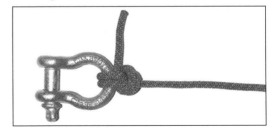

CAT'S PAW

An extremely strong hitch often used by dock workers, the Cat's Paw can be tied in the middle of a rope and placed over a rail or post. One of the main benefits of using the Cat's Paw is that, in theory, one of the weighted ends of the rope could break and the Cat's Paw would cinch down and hold the load in place with the remaining intact side of the rope.

1 Create a bight in the middle of the rope.

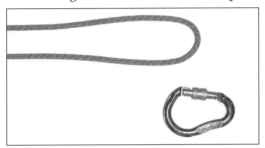

2 Fold the bight over to create two matching loops.

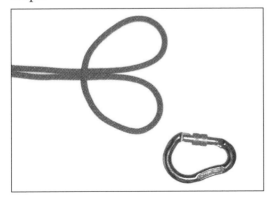

3 Twist the two loops in opposite directions (e.g., turn the left loop clockwise and the right loop counterclockwise).

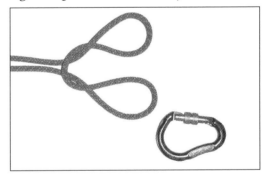

4 Continue twisting each loop until there are at least three twists in each side.

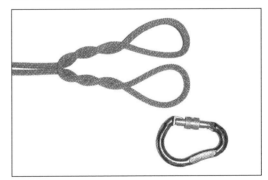

5 Insert a carabiner or other anchor point through the two loops.

6 Pull evenly and tighten until the knot is snug to the anchor point.

HIGHWAYMAN'S HITCH

The Highwayman's Hitch is a draw loop that is often used to secure a rope to an object that will need to be quickly released. When you're finished with the knot, you can simply pull on the working end and the knot will collapse. Because of this ease of release, it should never be used with a human load.

1 Make a bight in the rope and tuck it behind the object to which you are anchoring.

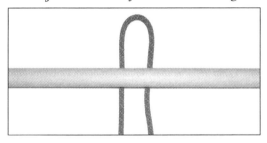

2 Create a second bight in the standing part of the rope and place it in front of the anchor.

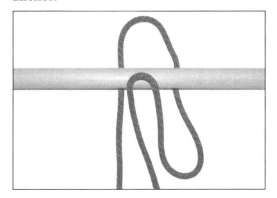

3 Tuck the second bight under the first (back) one and pull down on the working end.

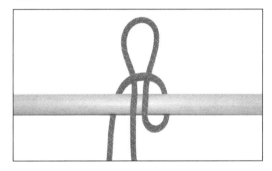

4 Make another bight (third total) in the working end.

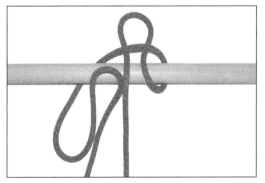

5 Tuck the third bight from front to back through the second bight.

6 Pull the standing part tightly to secure the knot.

ROLLING HITCH

Also known as: *Magnus Hitch, Magner's Hitch*

This is another variation of the Clove Hitch. It is not only used to attach ropes to an object, but is often used to attach a smaller diameter rope to a larger diameter rope. It is based on friction and was created to withstand a lengthwise pull.

1 Pass the working end of the rope around the object to which you are tying from front to back. Pull enough rope to wrap it again.

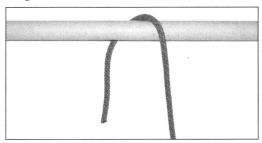

2 While holding the part of the rope that just passed around the object, cross the working end over the standing end.

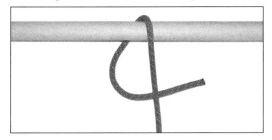

3 Wrap the working end around the object again going the same direction as the first loop, creating an "X."

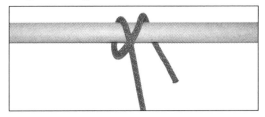

4 Wrap the working end around the object again, creating a second diagonal turn.

5 Tuck the working end underneath the final diagonal turn you just completed. Pull tight.

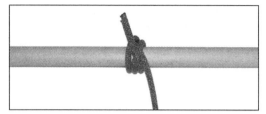

〰 KNOT NOTES 〰

Up until the turn of the 19th century, this knot was known as the Magnus Hitch. It was Richard Henry Dana Jr. who named it Rolling Hitch in his writing *The Seaman's Friend*, and the name has remained ever since.

HALTER HITCH

This is a variation of the Highwayman's Hitch that is often used to tie to the halters of animals, for example to a hitching post (though it is not uncommon for the animal to free itself by chewing the knot). It also has applications in hiking, climbing, and sailing, whenever there is a need to secure equipment or a boat to an object such as a dock in a way that enables it to be quickly and easily released.

1 Lead the working end through a ring or around an object and pass the working end around the standing end to form a second loop.

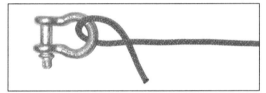

2 Create a bight in the working end and tuck it to create an Overhand Knot with a Draw Loop.

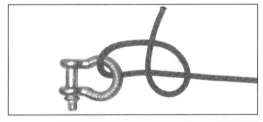

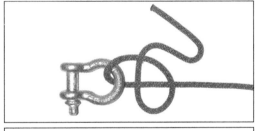

3 Pull tight.

PILE HITCH

Possibly the easiest hitch to tie, the Pile Hitch is so elementary that it isn't even considered a knot by some purists. It is ideally suited to tying cord to a post in a situation where the bight can be passed over the top of the post. This simple knot can be adapted into a variety of other knots such as a bend, binding, or loop.

1 Make a bight in the rope.

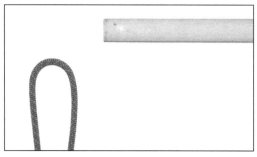

2 Wrap the bight around the post or object, passing the bight underneath both standing ends.

3 Pass the bight over the top of the post or object.

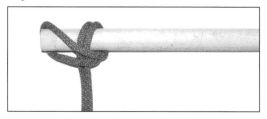

4 Pull tight.

DOUBLE PILE HITCH

John Smith, an active member of the International Guild of Knot Tyers, created this knot to secure a rope to an object and enable a lengthways pull.

1 Make a bight in the rope.

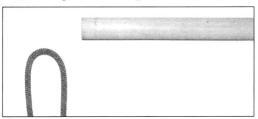

2 Wrap the bight around a post or object, passing the bight underneath both standing ends.

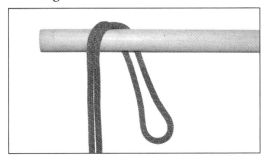

3 Wrap the bight around for one more full turn.

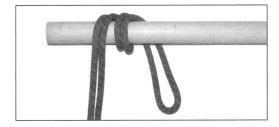

4 Place the bight over both standing parts and pass it over the post or object.

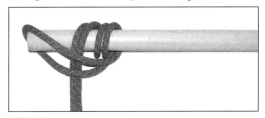

5 Pull tight.

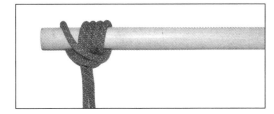

VIBRATION-PROOF HITCH

This hitch has ratchet-like qualities that make it a valuable knot when it is secured to a large diameter anchor and constant movement of the cord is an issue.

1 Pass the working end of the rope around an object.

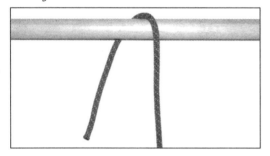

2 Cross the working end across the standing end, around the back side, and over the object again.

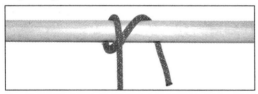

3 Bring the working end across the front of the standing part then through the first diagonal part from left to right.

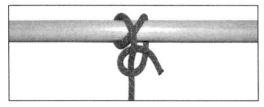

4 Continue the working end over the knot and tuck it under the upper portion of the first diagonal.

5 Pull tight.

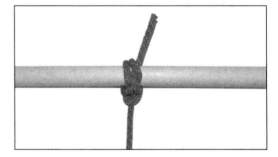

SNUGGLE HITCH

Yet another modification to the Clove Hitch, the Snuggle Hitch was first documented in 1987 and is an easy and secure way to fasten a rope to another rope, a pole, or any variety of anchor points. It provides greater security and strength than the Clove Hitch.

1 Pass the working end of the rope around the object to which you are tying and pull enough rope to wrap it again.

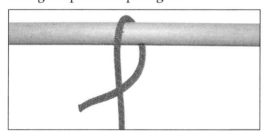

2 While holding the part of the rope that just passed around the object, cross the working end over the standing end and wrap the working end around the object again going the same direction as the first loop.

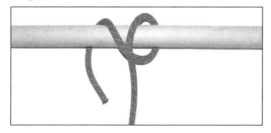

3 Tuck the working end under the part that crossed the working end.

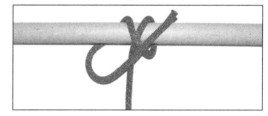

4 Bring the working end around the anchor once again.

5 Pass the working end over the near part of the knot and under the next.

6 Pass the working end down behind the back of the knot and to the front again.

8 Pull tight.

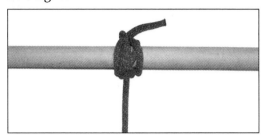

7 Tuck the working end over the near part of the knot and under the next.

BOOM HITCH

Also known as: *Decorative Hitch*

The Boom Hitch is popular due to its ease of tying and the fact that it can withstand tension at right angles as well as longitudinal pulls. Each turn simply wraps on top of the previous one; tighten carefully so as not to disturb the sequence of wraps.

1 Lay the working end diagonally across the anchor point.

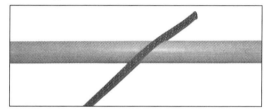

2 Wrap the working end around the anchor and bring it up across itself in front of the anchor, creating an "X."

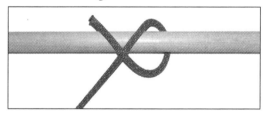

3 Wrap the working end around the anchor again.

4 Pass the working end diagonally across the wrap you just made in front of the anchor.

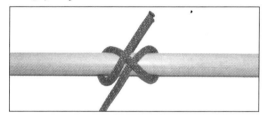

5 Wrap the working end around the anchor between the two existing knot parts.

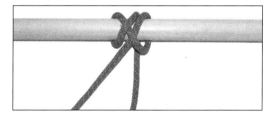

6 Bring the working end diagonally across the standing part of the rope.

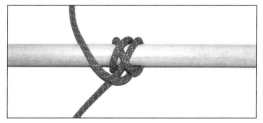

7 Pass the working end around the anchor once again.

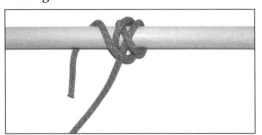

8 Make one final diagonal pass (left to right), passing over one part of the knot and tucking it under the next.

9 Pull tight.

◢◢◢ KNOT NOTES ◣◣◣

In his book *The Ashley Book of Knots*, Clifford Ashley called what is now known as the Boom Hitch the "Decorative Hitch."

LIGHTERMAN'S HITCH

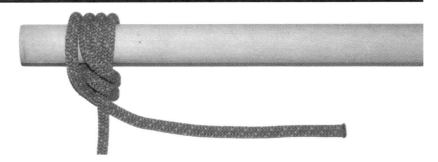

This hitch is popular in a variety of professions from longshoremen to theater stagehands. It is secure yet never completely tightens, which allows it to be quickly and easily untied. This hitch is unique in that no "knot" is actually tied. It uses friction wraps to withstand the load. The hitch can be loosened by unwrapping it, thus allowing the load to be lowered if desired.

1 Pass the working end of the rope around the anchor point.

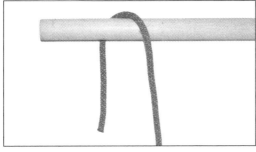

2 Complete a round turn around the anchor. (If tying the Lighterman's Hitch while the rope is weighted, the friction from the round turn should halt the weight of the load.)

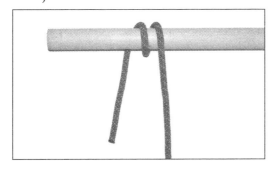

3 Create a bight in the working end.

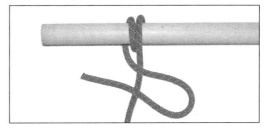

4 Tuck the bight beneath the standing part of the rope and over the anchor point.

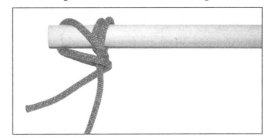

5 Wrap the working end around the standing part.

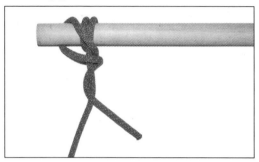

6 Create another bight in the working end and place it around the anchor again.

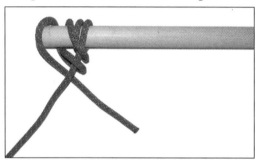

7 Repeat steps 5 and 6 as necessary.

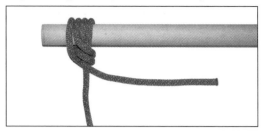

BALE SLING HITCH

Also known as: *Girth Hitch*

The Bale Sling Hitch is tied with a joined piece of rope and is possibly the easiest hitch to tie. It cinches down on the anchor and creates a handle or a point where you can tie or clip.

1 Pass the bight on one end of the rope around the object.

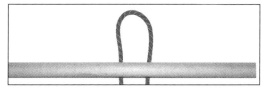

2 Tuck that bight beneath the bight at the other end of the rope.

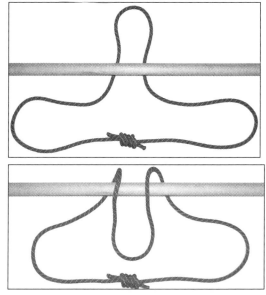

3 Pull tight.

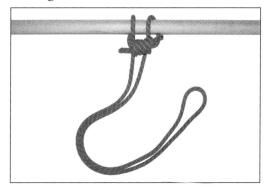

TIP

This hitch can be formed at the end of a loop knot such as a Double Fisherman.

RING HITCH

This hitch is most often used to attach an object to a lanyard. A piece of jewelry, a knife, a flashlight, or any other item can be secured with this simple hitch.

1 Place a bight in the rope and pass the bight through the eye of the object you want to secure.

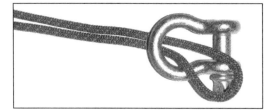

2 Spread the bight wide enough for it to pass over the object to which it is being secured.

3 Pass the bight over the object and pull the standing parts through the bight.

KNUTE HITCH

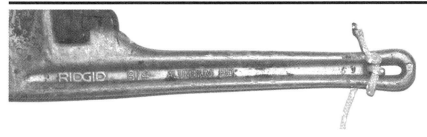

Another simple and handy way to attach a lanyard to an object is the Knute Hitch.

1 Tie a Figure Eight or similar stopper knot at the end of the rope.

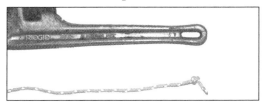

2 Form a bight in the rope.

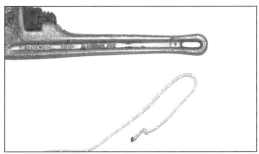

3 Pass it through the hole of the object to which you are securing it.

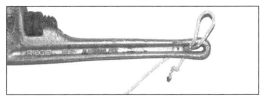

4 Pass the stopper knot you tied through the bight and pull the standing end.

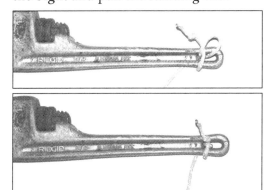

🪢 KNOT NOTES 🪢

The Knute Hitch was named in 1990 by rigger Brion Toss, who gave it the name after his favorite marlinspike (a tool used in marine ropework).

LOOPS

For as long as humans have needed to wrap a rope around a person or thing, there have been loops. These are knots where a loop is placed at the end of a line for any of a variety of uses. A loop can be used to hoist or pull loads, attach ropes to objects or people, or even create a handle. They can be dropped over or often tied around an object. Today most people tend to use manufactured safety rigging rather than tying loop knots, particularly in life safety applications, but it can still be useful to know how to tie them.

BOWLINE

Possibly the most famous of the loops, the bowline (pronounced boh-linn) is used for nearly every potential loop application. It maintains about 60 percent of the strength of the rope in which it is tied and does not slip, loosen, or jam. For added security a safety can be tied in the working end after tying the Bowline.

1 Make an underhand loop in the working end of the rope.

2 Bring the working end up through the loop. *Do not* pull tight; leave slack. This slack will become your loop.

3 Wrap the working end around the standing end. The strength of the knot will not be affected by which way you go around the standing end.

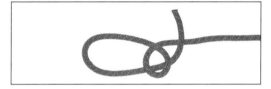

4 Tuck the working end back down into the loop.

5 Hold the working end along with the side of the loop next to it and pull the standing end to secure the knot.

///// KNOT NOTES \\\\\

This loop has long been taught to scouts, first responders, and outdoorsmen. An elementary method of teaching describes the working end as the tree, the loop as a rabbit hole, and the working end as the rabbit. The rabbit comes up out of the hole, around the tree, and back down into the hole.

DOUBLE BOWLINE

This is a reinforced version of the classic Bowline. It is significantly stronger than the already strong original version. Due to the strength of the knot and the extra wrap, a safety may not be necessary when tying the Double Bowline. It also has the advantage of being easy to untie.

1 Make an underhand loop in the working end of the rope.

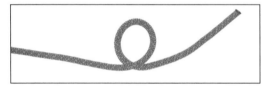

2 Make an identical loop above the first one.

3 Bring the working end up through the loop. *Do not* pull tight; leave slack. This slack will become your loop.

4 Wrap the working end around the standing end.

5 Tuck the working end back down into the loop.

6 Hold the working end along with the side of the loop next to it and pull the standing end to secure the knot.

WATER BOWLINE

This bowline is designed to be tied when the cord is wet. It is one of the more rugged versions of the Bowline and can withstand movement and dragging over rough terrain.

1 Make an underhand loop in the working end of the rope.

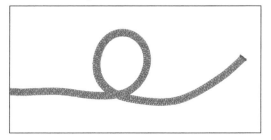

2 Bring the working end up through the loop. *Do not* pull tight; leave slack. This slack will become your loop.

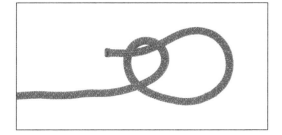

3 Create a second loop above and identical to the first.

4 Direct the working end up through the second loop.

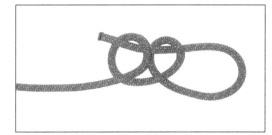

5 Wrap the working end around the standing end and tuck it back down through both loops.

6 Hold the working end along with the side of the loop next to it and pull the standing end to secure the knot.

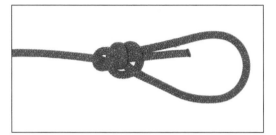

▰▰ TIP ▰▰

An easy way to tie the Water Bowline is to tie a Clove Hitch (see page 81) and tuck the working end up through both loops, around the standing end, and back down through the loops.

ANGLER'S LOOP

The Angler's Loop is, as you would guess, an old knot used by fisherman. It has gained favor due to its ability to remain tied and retain its strength in wet rope and even elastic/bungee cord. However, the Angler's Loop is prone to jamming and should not be used if the knot will need to be untied.

1 Make an overhand loop with the standing part of the rope.

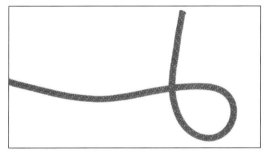

2 Lay the working end across the initial loop.

3 Pull a bight in the working end through the loop.

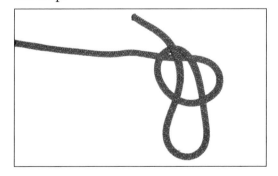

4 Wrap the working end around behind the standing end.

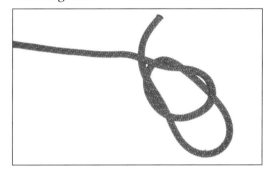

5 Pull the working end through the center of the knot and beneath the two legs of the loop.

6 Pull tight.

FIGURE OF EIGHT LOOP

Also known as: *Figure Eight Loop, Figure Eight on a Bight, Figure of Eight on a Bight, Flemish Loop, Flemish Eight*

While the Bowline is *the* timeless loop, this loop has gained popularity due to its strength and simplicity. Even young children just learning to tie knots can easily grasp the concept of a Figure of Eight Loop. It is used in caving, climbing, sailing, camping, and any other practical application you can imagine.

1 Place a bight in the rope.

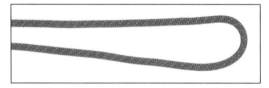

2 Fold the bight over (in essence creating another bight).

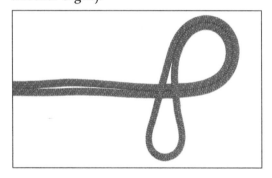

3 Wrap the bight one full time around both standing parts.

4 Tuck the bight through the top of the knot (the second bight you created in step 2).

5 Pull tight.

FIGURE OF EIGHT FOLLOW THROUGH

This loop will give you the same result as a Figure of Eight Loop, but can be tied around a stationary object. Although this is a secure knot, you should allow enough working end to tie an overhand knot around the working end as a safety once the knot is completed.

1 Tie a Figure of Eight in the rope with enough working end to wrap around your anchor and trace back through the knot.

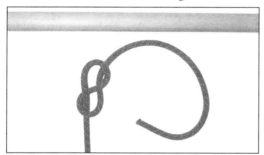

2 Wrap the working end around your anchor.

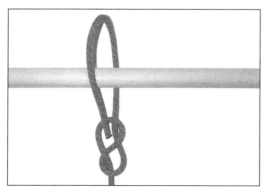

3 Place the working end against the standing end and trace the working end through the knot.

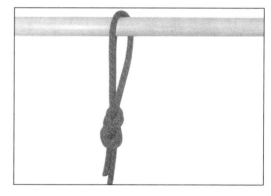

4 Dress the knot so the turns don't cross each other (make the knot "pretty").

5 Pull tight.

DOUBLE FIGURE OF EIGHT LOOP

Also known as: *Rescue Eight, Canadian Eight, Bunny Ears*

The Double Figure of Eight Loop is popular in climbing and rescue operations. It is a bulkier version of the Figure of Eight Loop and provides an extra loop to which one could tie in or clip a carabiner. Although it doesn't provide a significant increase in strength over the standard Figure of Eight Loop, its appearance can give you an extra feeling of security when operating in a vertical environment.

1 Place a bight in the rope.

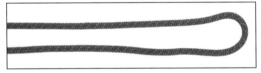

2 Fold the bight over (in essence creating another bight).

3 Wrap the bight one full time around both standing parts.

4 Place the bight around the back side and above the figure eight you just created.

5 Pull the two legs of the bight through the top loop.

7 Pull tight.

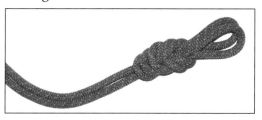

6 Pull the bight up and over the entire knot.

◢◢◢ TIP ◣◣◣

The loops of this knot can be used together by being tied or clipped into with a single carabiner, or each loop can be tied or clipped into separately.

TRIPLE
FIGURE OF EIGHT LOOP

Adding yet another anchor option to the Figure of Eight Loop, the Triple Figure of Eight offers even more opportunity by adding a third loop. The variety of loop options make it an attractive way to anchor a variety of loads. Caution should be used with this knot so as not to overweight the knot and the rope.

1 Place a bight in the rope.

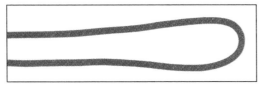

2 Fold the bight over (in essence creating another bight).

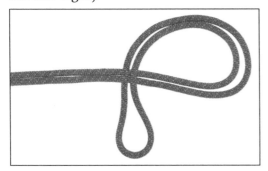

3 Wrap the bight one full time around both standing parts.

4 Place the bight around the back side and above the figure eight you just created.

5 Pull the two legs of the bight through the top loop.

6 Adjust the two legs to the loop sizes you require.

7 Lead the bight up and around the twin standing parts and tuck it back into the knot next to the two loops.

8 Tighten the knot so all three loops are the same size.

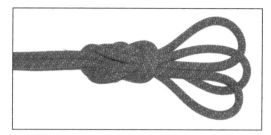

**//// TIP **

It takes a lot of rope to build this knot. When you fold over the initial bight (in step 2), give yourself more rope than you think you'll need. You can always adjust it later.

DIRECTIONAL FIGURE OF EIGHT

Also known as: *Inline Figure of Eight*

This knot is designed for situations where a loop is needed in the middle of the rope. It can assume a load in a single direction and functions as a noose by tightening as it is weighted.

1 Create a bight in the middle of the rope.

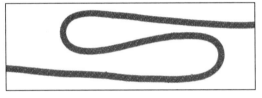

2 Pass the bight over the standing end.

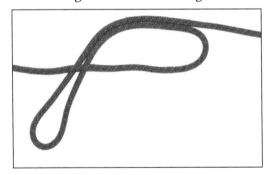

3 Bring the bight around the standing end.

4 Tuck the bight into the opening.

5 Pull tight.

〰️ TIP 〰️

The Directional Figure of Eight must be facing the direction in which the load will be pulling. A pull in the opposite direction will capsize, constrict, and weaken the knot.

FARMER'S LOOP

The Farmer's Loop was documented in 1912 as a knot used to tie loops on American farms. It is a quick and easy way to tie a loop into the middle of a rope. After you learn how to tie this loop, it becomes second nature and is one of the quicker loops you can tie.

1 Drape the rope over your hand near your thumb.

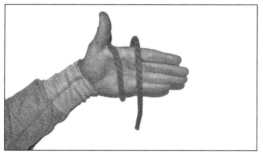

2 Wrap the rope around your hand, from back to front, two more times.

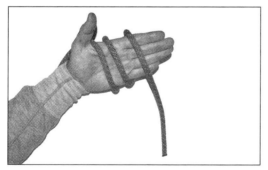

3 Raise the middle loop and place it over the right loop.

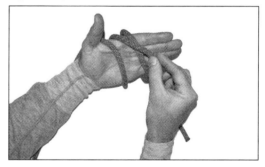

4 Raise the "new" middle loop and place it over the left loop.

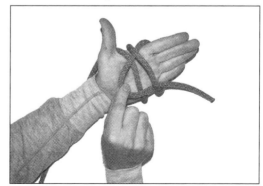

5 Raise the "new" middle loop and lay it over the right loop again.

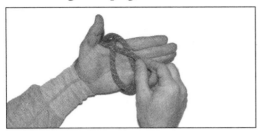

6 Pull the "new" middle loop and withdraw your hand.

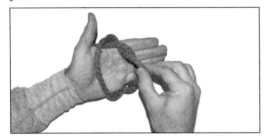

7 Work the knot by pulling the loop and the two working ends individually until the knot is secure.

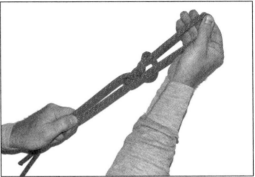

⫸⫸⫸ KNOT NOTES ⫷⫷⫷

This knot was documented by Howard Riley, a Cornell University professor, who was shown the knot by a farmer at the Genesee County Fair in New York in 1910.

BLOOD LOOP DROPPER KNOT

This loop is commonly used by fishermen, particularly fly fishermen, who maintain that this knot should be only be used for fishing line. However, when used with thicker cords, it can provide a way to attach a variety things to rope for basic utility purposes.

1 Place a loop in the rope.

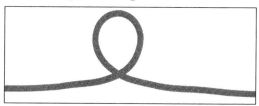

2 Tuck the working end through the loop, creating an overhand knot.

3 Continue to tuck the working end through the loop, creating wraps.

4 Do this a minimum of three times (which is a Triple Overhand Knot as seen on page 17).

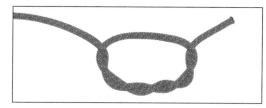

5 Tuck the top center of the knot down through the middle wrap.

6 Work and shape the two sides of the knot until they are snug and secure.

〰〰 KNOT NOTES 〰〰

Some sources say the term "blood" in knots traces back to the knot that was tied in the end of a whiplash because of its ability to draw blood. Others say it is from the bleeding fingers that would often occur when repeatedly tying it in fishing lines.

BOWSTRING KNOT

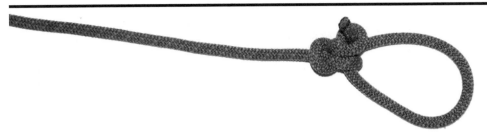

Also known as: *Honda Knot*

The Bowstring Knot is a simple loop. Though not strong enough to be used in life safety situations, it is a good knot for small tasks. It is most commonly used to tie the sliding loop on the lassos of cowboys. Its main drawback is that, once weighted, it becomes extremely difficult, if not impossible, to untie.

1 With the working end of the rope, tie an Overhand Knot.

2 Bring the working end through the top part of the knot (as shown).

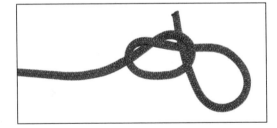

3 Tie an Overhand Knot as a safety in the working end.

4 Pull tight.

〰 KNOT NOTES 〰

This knot was used by Elizabethan archers, who looped the top of their bowstrings and pulled them tight with the Bowstring Knot.

ALPINE BUTTERFLY

Also known as: *Butterfly, Butterfly Knot, Lineman's Loop, Lineman's Rider*

The Alpine Butterfly is the single most used loop when a three-way pull is needed. A three-way pull is when tension is applied to both ends of the rope and a knot is weighted in the middle of the rope. For example, a rope is tied between two trees and a knot is tied in the middle so a carabiner can be clipped in to keep your food bag from animals. The Alpine Butterfly can easily be tied in the working part of the rope, and it is strong and secure. It also has the benefit of enabling you to remove the worn part of a rope from the inline strength by placing the worn part on the bight extending out of the knot.

1 Drape the rope over your open hand at an angle extending away from your thumb.

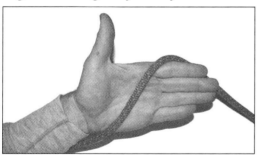

2 Bring the rope around and over the front of the hand, crossing the first wrap and forming an "X."

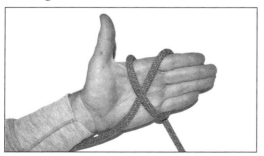

3 Continue wrapping one more time around the hand, working closer to the thumb.

4 Pull slack in the "center" of the three wraps and lay the loose rope on your hand facing back toward your wrist.

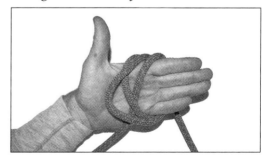

5 Tuck that loop under the "X" toward your fingertips.

6 Withdraw your hand from the knot and pull the standing ends in one direction and the bight in the other.

7 The knot is complete when you pull the two standing ends apart from each other, popping the knot into its final position.

〰 KNOT NOTES 〰

There are multiple ways to tie the Alpine Butterfly, and those proficient in tying it tend to be loyal to their method. The steps listed here describe one of the more common ways to tie it.

ARTILLERY LOOP

Also known as: *Manharness Knot, Manharness Hitch, Harness Loop*

This loop is used for small jobs that are not critical for life safety. The Artillery Loop is made for a three-way pull in which a load is pulled perpendicular to the rope. It can be quickly tied in the standing part of a rope and is best used for light and temporary purposes such as tying the leash of a small animal or securing gear to a rope to prevent it from sliding or floating away.

1 Make a loop in the standing part of a rope.

2 Fold the loop over and across one of the standing ends so that it can be seen in the loop. (Depending on which way you made your loop, only one standing end will be correct. This will be obvious because if you go to the wrong side, the knot will fall apart in your hand.)

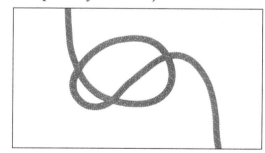

3 Reach underneath the standing part and pull the top of the loop up through the center of the knot.

4 Pull tight.

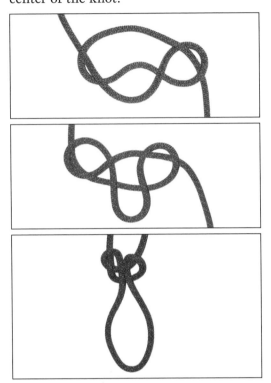

⚓ KNOT NOTES ⚓

The name of this knot has its origins in the military, where it was used to haul field artillery into position. The same knot, also known as the Harness Loop, is historically used to tether horses, particularly when traversing challenging terrain.

ADJUSTABLE LOOP

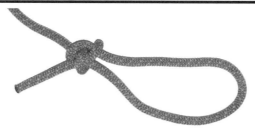

The Adjustable Loop can easily be altered by sliding the knot up and down the standing end to make the loop smaller or larger. It is commonly used when there is a need (and the means) to quickly place a loop over an object. It will automatically cinch down on the object when the standing end is pulled. There is a built-in safety attribute that allows the knot to slide and grip when placed under a shock load until friction can stop it.

1 Create an Overhand Loop in the rope.

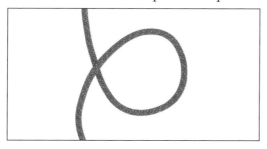

2 Tuck the working end through the loop.

3 Tuck the working end through a second time.

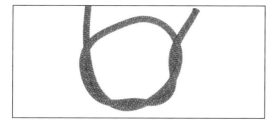

4 Pass the working end around both legs of the loop.

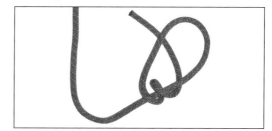

5 Tuck the working end beneath the second (final) wrap.

6 Pull tight.

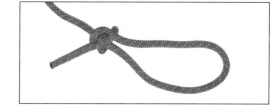

WATER KNOT

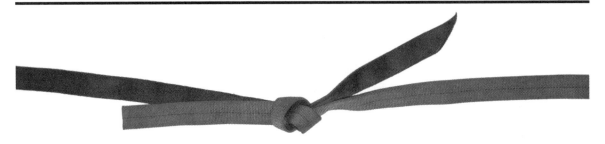

Every knot listed in this book is for cordage, but since webbing is a significant tool used by many preppers, it's worth mentioning the Water Knot. This is the best way to join webbing, whether you want to tie two pieces of webbing together or tie webbing to itself. You may find yourself in a situation where you need to join multiple small pieces of webbing to create a bigger one, or where you need to tie webbing around an object. This knot maintains the majority of the strength of webbing and is simple to tie.

1 Tie an Overhand Knot in the first piece of webbing.

2 Place the working end of the second piece of webbing (or the other end of the first piece) against the working end of the first.

3 By placing the second working end flat against the first, begin tracing the Overhand Knot.

4 Continue tracing it throughout the knot.

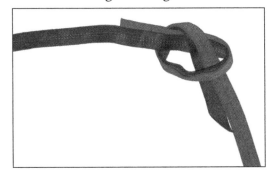

5 Once you have traced it all the way through, pull the pieces of webbing in opposing directions to tighten.

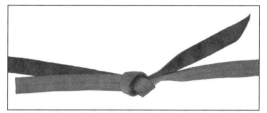

▰▰▰ TIP ▰▰▰

You'll know you have it right when the Water Knot looks like an Overhand Knot with a tail sticking out of either end. You can tie safety knots in the working ends sticking out of the sides, but most experts say it isn't necessary with this knot.

ARBOR KNOT

This is a common knot used by fishermen when attaching monofilament line to a reel (also known as an arbor). It can be tied in cord as a secure slip knot, but garners its most use in fishing applications. In a camping or survival situation, this knot can be used to attach fishing line to a stick, even a large one.

1 Create a bight in the rope.

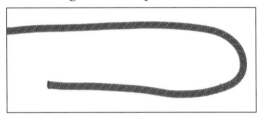

2 Tie an Overhand Knot around the standing end of the rope, creating a simple Slip Knot, and tighten the knot around the standing end.

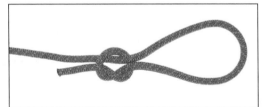

3 Tie another Overhand Knot in the end of the working end.

4 Pull the standing end until the knot tightens onto itself.

TOM FOOL'S KNOT

Also known as: *Conjurer's Knot*

A simple handcuff-style knot, the Tom Fool's Knot has been used in a variety of situations from rescue, to prisoner constraint, to hobbling the legs of livestock.

1 Put two loops in the rope side by side, one clockwise and one counterclockwise.

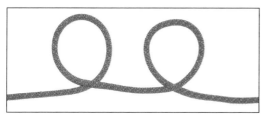

2 Partially overlap the two loops with the clockwise loop on top (at this point the knot will look like a pretzel).

3 Pull the leading edge of the clockwise loop through the back of the knot and the counterclockwise loop through the front.

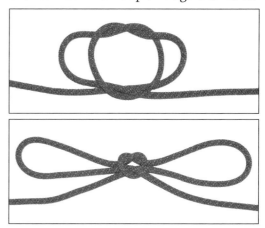

HANDCUFF KNOT

Also known as: *Hobble Knot*

This is similar to the Tom Fool's Knot, differing only in the way the final loops are created. It can be used in the exact same way but is arguably slightly stronger. Despite the name, this knot does not have any sort of locking action, but is simply two adjustable loops in opposing directions.

1 Put two loops in the rope side by side, one clockwise and one counterclockwise.

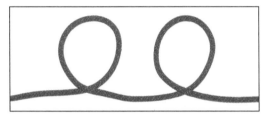

2 Partially overlap the two loops with the clockwise loop on the bottom (at this point the knot will look like a pretzel).

3 Pull the leading edge of the clockwise loop through the back of the knot and the counterclockwise loop through the front.

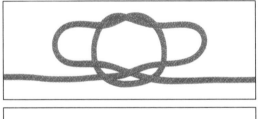

⫻⫻⫻ TIP ⫻⫻⫻

Use caution when using this knot for rescue purposes. When placed over a victim's hands, the knot will cinch down on their wrists, but the danger comes when the would-be rescuer begins to pull. The weight of the victim is often enough to cause further injury even as the victim is pulled to safety.

FIREMAN'S CHAIR KNOT

Also known as: *Chair Knot, Man-O-War Sheepshank*

The Fireman's Chair Knot is a makeshift harness used to support the torso and the legs of a victim as they are moved to safety. It is an extension of the Handcuff Knot made with much larger bights. If this knot is being tied to carry a person, use great caution to make sure it is tied correctly.

1 Put two loops in the rope side by side, one clockwise and one counterclockwise.

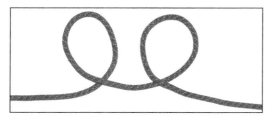

2 Partially overlap the two loops with the clockwise loop on the bottom (at this point the knot will look like a pretzel).

3 Pull the leading edge of the clockwise loop through the back of the knot and the counterclockwise loop through the front.

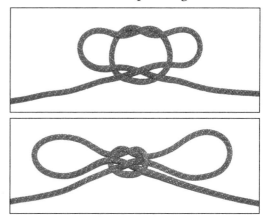

4 Twist the working end of one side of the knot into a Half Hitch and wrap it around the bight on the same side, so that the working end is in front of the knot, placing it snugly against the center of the knot.

5 Twist the working end of the other side of the knot into a Half Hitch and wrap it around the bight on the same side, so that the working end is in front of the knot, also placing it snugly against the center of the knot.

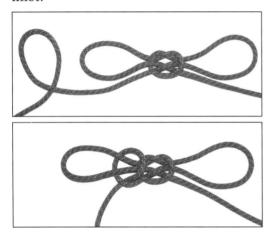

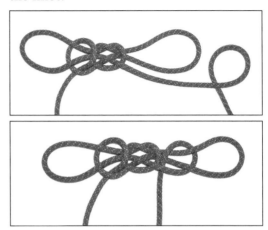

⬤⬤ TIP ⬤⬤

Understand that this application is very uncomfortable for the person being moved to safety. It should be used only when absolutely necessary.

HANGMAN'S NOOSE

Also known as: *Hangman's Knot, Jack Ketch Knot*

The Hangman's Noose is one of the most visually identifiable knots, mostly due to the gruesome purpose that gives it its name. Most people shy away from using this knot because of its history, but despite its dark reputation, the Hangman's Noose is actually a very strong and secure loop knot that can be used in fishing, boating, and a variety of other applications. It can easily be untied by simply pulling the working end through the coils.

1 Create a bight in a rope toward the end.

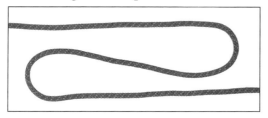

2 Create another bight on the working-end side of the first bight. Depending on the size of the knot you want, each bight should be approximately 8–10 inches long. The working end should be longer than your two bights.

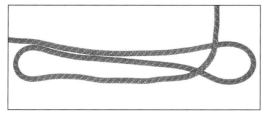

3 Grasp the two bights together, leaving the working end loose (you should have a bight at the top and a bight at the bottom).

4 Begin wrapping the working end around the initial bight, making sure the wraps are very tight.

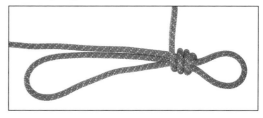

5 Continue wrapping until you run out of rope.

6 Tuck the remaining working end through the bight at the end of your turns.

7 Pull the bottom bight to tighten and secure the knot.

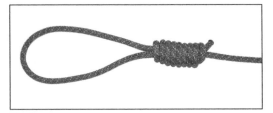

///// KNOT NOTES \\\\\

Urban legend states that there should be 13 loops for it to be a true Hangman's Noose, but as long as there are more than three wraps, it will perform.

MUNTER HITCH

Also known as: *Italian Hitch, Crossing Hitch, HMS*

The Munter Hitch is a friction hitch, which by definition is a knot that is tied around itself or another rope in such a way that it that allows up and down movement, but remains stationary when placed under a load. It is commonly used to rappel or, more commonly, belay (safety) in synthetic ropes. It is popular among climbers, arborists, and rescuers. It is typically tied around a locking carabiner. If you need to quickly rappel or lower something, the Munter Hitch can be tied in seconds and put into action.

1 Cross one end of the rope over the other.

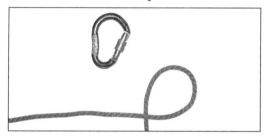

2 Fold the loop you just created down over where the ropes cross, creating a bight.

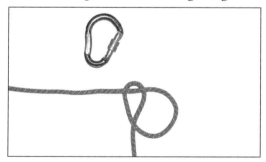

3 Clip your carabiner around the twin legs of the bight.

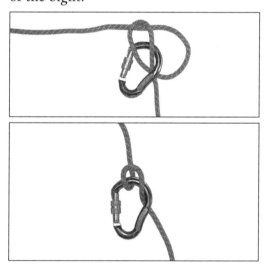

⬛⬛ KNOT NOTES ⬛⬛

The Munter Hitch is also known as the HMS, which is an abbreviation for *Halbmastwurfsicherung*, which in some translations means "half clove hitch belay."

DOUBLE MUNTER HITCH

The Munter Hitch is an extremely popular hitch, but when the weight of the load is substantial, a Double Munter Hitch is often used. The extra wrap creates additional friction, allowing the weight of the load to be better controlled.

1 Cross one end of the rope over the other.

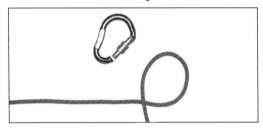

2 Create an additional loop right next to the one created in Step 1.

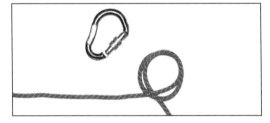

3 Fold the loop you just created down over where the ropes cross, creating a bight.

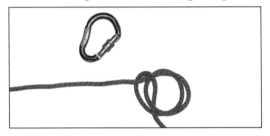

4 Clip your carabiner through the hitch.

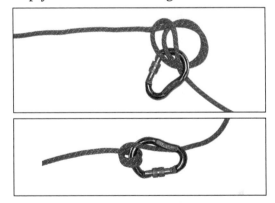

💨 KNOT NOTES 💨

The Double Munter Hitch was first documented by Canadian climber Robert Chisnall. It is ideal for smaller diameter rope where more friction is needed.

PRUSIK

The Prusik is a simple and time-tested way to attach a smaller diameter rope to a larger diameter rope. It is used to halt the progress of rope, tie an object to a rope, or even ascend a rope by using two additional ropes. Attach two long Prusiks (about three feet each in length) to the rope you wish to climb. Place a foot in each Prusik loop and alternate sliding the loops up the main rope. It will take some coordination but in this way you can actually take steps up a rope.

1 Put a bight in the rope.

2 Wrap the bight around the larger diameter rope.

3 Pass the standing end through the bight.

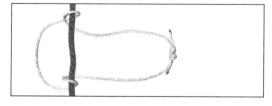

4 Pass the standing end through the bight again.

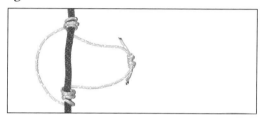

5 Pull the bight to tighten the knot.

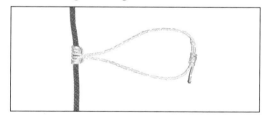

 **KNOT NOTES**

The Prusik was originally devised by Australian music professor Dr. Karl Prusik, who created it to repair the broken strings of musical instruments during World War I.

COILS

Coiling a rope is a term used to describe tidying up an unattached rope in an organized fashion. Most often a person will grab a rope in their hand and wrap it around their elbow and back to their hand over and over until the entirety of the rope is wrapped into a "coil." While this is possibly the easiest way to arrange an unattached rope for either organization or transport, it is not the best. That method often leaves twists in the rope that become entangled and create a headache for the person trying to use the rope.

A better method is to place one end of the rope between your left thumb and forefinger. Grab the rope with your right hand about 3 feet away with both palms down. With your right hand, place the rope between your thumb and forefinger. Next bring your right hand to your left hand so the tips of your thumbs meet and the newly created loop forms towards your left wrist. At the same time, roll the rope in your right hand between your thumb and forefinger away from you. Now grab it with your left hand and slide your right hand down the rope another 3 feet and repeat until only 2 or 3 feet remain, which will be used to wrap the rope and finalize the coil.

ALPINE COIL

The Alpine Coil, used to secure coiled rope for storage or transport, is a favorite among climbers. It is easy to learn, tie, and untie.

1 Hold the top of your coiled rope, bringing the two ends together.

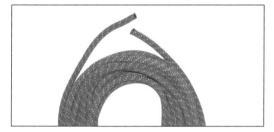

2 Create a small bight in one end.

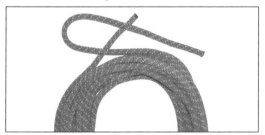

3 Uncoil one loop of the other end and begin tightly wrapping the top of the coil at the beginning of the bight you created, working toward the bight itself.

4 Once you reach the end of the rope, tuck it into the wrapped bight.

5 Pull the other end of the bight, which will secure the knot.

FIGURE OF EIGHT COIL

This coiling method is quick, easy, and simple to untie when the rope is needed in a hurry. You expedite the process by doubling the rope prior to coiling, and it ends up with a practical loop for hanging.

1 Locate the middle of the rope and coil it doubled.

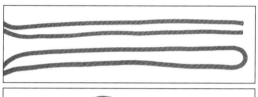

2 Once completely coiled, bring the bight one full turn around the coil.

3 Tuck the bight under the top of the coil.

4 Pull tight.

FIREMAN'S COIL

Another popular way to coil a rope is the Fireman's Coil. The main benefit of this coil is that it not only keeps your rope organized and secure, but can be released by a simple pull of the end of the rope.

1 Coil the rope.

2 Bring the two ends together.

3 With one end, make a large Overhand Loop.

4 Run the working end through the coil and behind it, creating another bight.

5 Tuck the second bight up through the first.

6 Pull tight.

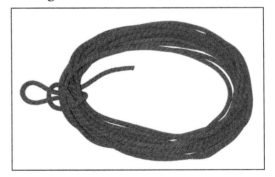

DAISY CHAIN

The Daisy Chain is a popular way to organize and store webbing and sometimes rope for quick deployment. The Daisy Chain is fun because it looks like a large mess of knots but easily comes undone if you simply pull one end or shake it loose.

1 Locate the center point in the rope.

2 Create a Half Hitch.

3 Pull both legs of the standing end up through the loop in the Half Hitch just enough to make a bight.

4 While holding the newly formed bight, pull the standing end and the bight with the two rope ends.

5 Place the two working parts of the rope up into the bight just far enough to make another bight.

6 Continue tucking the two working parts of the rope up into the most recently formed bight just enough to create another bight.

7 Do this until the entire rope is chained.

INDEX OF KNOTS

ACKNOWLEDGMENTS

I would like to thank all at Ulysses Press, particularly Casie Vogel and Bridget Thoreson, for your hard work, patience, and feedback, and the design team who made this book what it has become. As always, thank you to my family, my sons Ryan, Nicholas, and Cameron, and to Scott B. Williams. A huge thanks to Amy Wewers for putting in the hours and dedication to getting the pictures just right, and for keeping me inspired. And to Wiley Wewers for her ever vigilant, watchful eye.

ABOUT THE AUTHOR

Scott Finazzo has been a firefighter for nearly 20 years and is currently serving as a lieutenant for the Overland Park, Kansas, Fire Department. He has been an instructor for firefighting tactics, confined space rescue, first aid, CPR, Community Emergency Response Teams, and other emergency training. In addition to being an emergency responder and educator, Scott has been writing in various capacities for much of his life, contributing to blogs, magazines, and books. Scott's first book, coauthored with Scott B. Williams, *The Prepper's Workbook*, became a national best seller. He followed that up with the narrative of his kayak journey through the Virgin Islands called *Why Do All the Locals Think We're Crazy?* Most recently he wrote *The Neighborhood Emergency Response Handbook* and *The Prepper's Survival Medicine Handbook*.

Scott has a bachelor's degree in management and human relations, and two associate degrees. Follow him at www.scottfinazzo.com.